History of Cuba

A Captivating Guide to Cuban History, Starting from Christopher Columbus' Arrival to Fidel Castro

Free Bonus from Captivating History (Available for a Limited time)

Hi History Lovers!

Now you have a chance to join our exclusive history list so you can get your first history ebook for free as well as discounts and a potential to get more history books for free! Simply visit the link below to join.

Contents

INTRODUCTION 1

CHAPTER 1 – CUBA BEFORE COLUMBUS 3

CHAPTER 2 – THE ARRIVAL OF THE SPANIARDS 9

CHAPTER 3 – SLAVERY AND SUGARCANE 19

CHAPTER 4 – WAR 27

CHAPTER 5 – THE CRY OF YARA 40

CHAPTER 6 – FREEDOM...48

CHAPTER 7 – INDEPENDENT AT LAST 57

CHAPTER 8 – A NEW LEADER 65

CHAPTER 9 – CASTRO'S CUBA...75

CHAPTER 10 – DESPERATE TIMES 81

CHAPTER 11 – A NEW HORIZON 88

CONCLUSION 92

SOURCES 98

Introduction

Do not fear a glorious death/because to die for the country is to live [...] hear the clarion call/Hasten, brave ones, to battle!

The words of "La Bayamesa," Cuba's national anthem, ring with so many of the qualities of the Cuban people, as they have proven time and time again during their long, bloody, and courageous history. Fearlessness, community, and passion are among them; Cuba has stared death in the face throughout its rocky history, and most of the time it has gazed into the eyes of death and smiled.

Over and over, oppressors have attempted to seize this island and its riches for their own selfish purposes; over and over, revolutions have risen up to conquer in an attempt to return Cuba to its people.

This started as early as the beginning of the sixteenth century, when Spanish conquistadors came to butcher the peaceful Taíno. A Taíno chief named Hatuey rose against them, and although his defense ultimately failed, he defied the Spanish to the end even as they burned him at the stake. In the eighteenth century, a Spanish officer named Luis Vicente de Velasco would suffer a similar fate as he stood against the British in a battle that he knew he would never win, nevertheless fighting to the death rather than surrendering to the baying hordes. At last, a legion of heroes—starting with a man who rang a slave bell, not to call his slaves to work, but to set them free—would rise up during three wars of independence, fighting not only for freedom but for racial equality. It would take generations, but eventually, these heroes would throw off their chains and win.

Finally, the famous Fidel Castro would rise to power in a valiant struggle of hundreds versus hundreds of thousands, in an unlikely victory that was hard fought for and hard won. He would change Cuba from a country that had been called an American colony in everything but name to one of America's most terrifying threats during the Cold War.

The story of Cuba is a tale of courage and sacrifice, of horrific oppression and inspiring vision. It is a story about exploitation and hope, about a tiny island that rose to global importance. There are battles and shipwrecks, pirates and Indians, tragic sacrifices and resounding triumphs. The Cuban people over and over show their resilience, courage, and passion in the face of incredible odds. They are a people that one cannot help but admire. And this is their story.

Chapter 1 – Cuba before Columbus

Atabei was before all things, and by Atabei all things were created. She was the powerful mother of the world. And for centuries, there was no sound, nor was there light. The world slept deeply in a silent darkness that ached with loneliness. And Atabei, moving through the slumbering universe, felt that loneliness with a keen agony.

Finally, she realized what was missing Life that was not just her own. So, she reached into the depths of the universe and seized magical, invisible, mystical elements in her hands, weaving them together to create living beings other than herself. She called them her sons; they were born simultaneously, perfect twins, none older than the other. She named them Yucajú and Guacar, and the mother of the earth was no longer lonely.

But Yucajú felt that something was still missing. He searched and searched through the dark and unmoving world, and could not discover that which could quell the yearning in his heart. So, he stood above the earth and he created the blazing sun, and the sun brought forth light. The light stretched out across the world, and wherever it touched, it brought life. Yucajú made the moon, but its light was too feeble to illuminate the night, so he gathered armfuls of precious stones and flung them into the sky; they shone where they stuck, and he named them stars.

The light of the sun and moon coaxed the earth to bring forth grass and trees and all green things. Then Yucajú made animals and birds to populate the earth and sea. They swarmed across the world, bringing noise to the earth, and there was life. But it was still not enough for him. One last piece was missing. one final creation that would make the world everything that Yucajú wanted it to be. It was not an animal, and it was not a god. It was halfway in between, and Yucajú named it Locuo. He was the first man.

He was the first soul.

- Taíno creation myth

Thousands of years ago, living in caves and chipping away at the world with tools made of shells, the Guanahatabey inhabited an island that would later be known as Cuba. But in 3000 BC, Cuba didn't have a name, or if it did, it was lost along with the Guanahatabey language.

Cuba's history does not begin with Columbus. Thousands of years before the Spanish would even set eyes on its idyllic shore. The island was populated with complex societies of indigenous peoples.

The First Cubans

Much of the Guanahatabey culture is lost to the mists of time. What little we do know about them comes from brief snippets in reports from 15th-century explorers and from archaeological sites, the oldest one being Levisa, which dates back nearly five thousand years. We do know that these peaceful, primitive people had little in the way of tools or agriculture. They did not have steel or ceramic; instead, they used shells for cutting, eating, and digging. They did not grow any of their own food. They were a gathering and fishing tribe who took what they needed from the world around them.

Apparently unable to build houses, the Guanahatabey tribe often slept under the stars, seeking shelter from the Caribbean hurricanes in caves. Their favorite food was mollusks, supplemented by fish and fruit. They neither hunted nor really fought, and when the Taíno came, they were utterly unprepared.

It's not entirely certain where the Taíno came from; the Amazon Basin is one possibility, and the Colombian Andes another. Either way, when they migrated to modern-day Cuba, the Guanahatabey were swept aside. The Taíno came in vast numbers and bore all kinds of tools and advancements that the Guanahatabey had no concept of, including dugout canoes, houses, and spears. There appears to have been little resistance. The Guanahatabey simply melted away in the face of the Taíno tide, and not for the last time, Cuba was overrun with a new people.

The Era of the Taíno

The Guanahatabey didn't stand a chance against the Taíno, and for good reason. This was a far more advanced people with an organized society that included chiefs, villages, a complex religion, and even ball games.

The Taíno lived in villages consisting of picturesque round houses with thatched roofs known as bohios; Cuban farmers still construct similar houses today. All the Taíno lived in these bohios except for the caciques, or chiefs. Caciques lived in rectangular houses called caneys, which set them apart from the common people. The people were further divided into nataínos, nobles who functioned as sub-caciques, and naborias, who were the lower classes and performed most of the work overseen by nataínos.

Caciques were also assisted by behiques, who were the spiritual leaders and medicine men of the village. Residents of the village would go to the behiques for advice or supernatural aid. Both caciques and behiques were generally male, but if male heirs couldn't be found, women could also become caciques; however, there are no records of female behiques. In fact, Taíno women were fairly independent and held considerable power in their society. Even married women slept in separate buildings from the men, staying in groups of other women and children; this gave them considerable independence and freedom to do as they pleased much of the time. The Taíno also had gender roles: men generally would hunt, while women grew crops and wove cotton into hammocks and aprons. Children commonly gathered shellfish, which was not as important in the Taíno diet as it was in that of the Guanahatabey.

The most important food for the Taíno was yuca. This tuberous root was meticulously cultivated, then harvested, grated, squeezed of its poisonous juices, and ground into flour. The resultant cassava bread lasted for months, even in the humidity of the Caribbean climate. Other crops included cotton, corn, sweet potatoes, and tobacco.

Taíno spent most of their time working in their fields. They were a peaceable people, with only small skirmishes occurring between neighboring chiefs. In fact, much of the time squabbles were not settled by battle, but by ball games.

These games were played on small, flat plazas located at the center of each village. Known as *batey*, the game was played with a bouncy, rubber-like ball. It appears to have been something similar to volleyball, except that players were not allowed to touch the ball with their hands. The game was played between two teams of up to thirty people, sometimes consisting of opposing tribes who would use it to settle disputes without resorting to warfare. This use of a ball game instead of battle was typical of the Taíno's fun and peace-loving nature.

When arguments couldn't be settled by *batey*, a more aggressive approach had to be taken. Taíno warfare was not highly organized, nor was weapons crafted with great care. Their weapon of choice was a wooden club/spear hybrid called a *macana*, which was only about an inch think, but sharp enough to be dangerous.

At the time of Columbus' arrival in Cuba, the island was divided into twenty-nine small chiefdoms presided over by the caciques who required tribute from the people over whom they ruled. Many of the places in Cuba still retain their Taíno names, such as Havana,

Bayamo, and Baracoa. In fact, the name "Cuba" is derived from a Taíno word, although it's unclear what exactly the word meant; it probably meant "fertile land."

Where Did the Taíno Come From?

Scholars are in dispute over the actual origins of the Taíno. The most likely theory is that they came from the center of the Amazon Basin, migrating along the island chains until they reached Cuba, Puerto Rico, and Jamaica. The counterargument, known as the circum-Caribbean theory, is that they came from Colombian Andes and from there migrated through the islands and eventually into Central and South America.

Which of these theories is correct has still not been proven. But the Taíno themselves have their own explanation of their origins in the form of their creation story about love, treachery, and loneliness that reflects this forgotten people's passionate emotion and simple practicality—qualities that characterize the Cuban people to this day.

Taíno mythology is rich and complex. They worshiped idols carved from stone and wood, which represented gods and ancestors, and were known as zemís. Atabei remained the greatest power in their mythology, but her and Yucajú's benevolent presence was countered by that of the god of evil. Originally called Guacar, he was Yucajú's twin brother. Jealous of the things Yucajú had created, Guacar turned to evil and changed his name to Juracán. His special power was wind, and the Taíno blamed him for their one great enemy: hurricanes. In fact, the word "hurricane" is derived from Juracán's name.

Other Indigenous Cubans

After the Guanahatabey dwindled to nearly nothing, Cuba was populated by the Taíno and other nations grouped under the Arawak label, which included many indigenous peoples of Central and South America and the Caribbean. The Classic Taíno—the most common subgroup of the Taíno people—lived throughout the western part of Cuba, while central Cuba was populated mostly by the Ciboney. The

Ciboney were a similar group of people to the Taíno, but not as advanced. They lived in harmony alongside their more sophisticated neighbors, and later, they would be persecuted alongside them, too.

Both of these groups thrived in Cuba's nurturing climate. They spread out and populated almost all of the island, numbering about 350,000 by the end of the fifteenth century. Their only real enemy was the hurricanes that had always wrought havoc on the islands; apart from this, they lived in peace and freedom, free to express their unique culture and honor their centuries-old tradition.

But soon all that would change. The Spanish were coming.

Chapter 2 – The Arrival of the Spaniards

Hidden behind a sand dune on the beach, a young Taíno watched in awe as the giant canoe grew closer and closer on the horizon. When it had first emerged as a mere speck out to sea, he had wondered if it could have been a sea monster. As it grew closer and he saw that it was a vessel, he crouched, ready to run back to the village and sound the alarm: the only people who came here from over the sea were the marauding Caribs, servants of Juracán who sought only to kill, plunder, and enslave. But something kept him watching as the great canoe drew closer, and it became evident that this was no Carib raiding party. This canoe was unlike anything he'd ever seen before. It was not rowed; instead, it seemed to move forward of its own accord. It had a series of great white wings that were spread wide in the wind, yet it didn't fly. Instead, it skimmed across the water towards the island, swift, powerful, and massive. The young man knew that the chief's canoe—the biggest in the village—could carry fifty people. But this one was on a scale he could barely even comprehend. Hundreds must be able to fit into it. His entire village could fit in it.

The great canoe drew nearer, and for the first time, the young man caught a glimpse of its occupants. For a long time, he could only stare in wonder. He had never seen anything like them before. They wore strange cloths over their bodies, which covered their arms and legs almost entirely; their hair was not long and coarse like his own, but close-cropped and curly. And skin. It was as pale as the moon, far paler his own.

A wild hope formed in the young man's mind. Just as the murdering Caribs were the servants of the god of evil, he knew that Yucajú had servants too, people who existed to help and to heal. Perhaps Yucajú had sent these people to help them, to protect them from the Caribs. As the great canoe slowed in the bay, the young Taíno leaped to his feet and ran back to the village to bring them the great news. The servants of Yucajú had arrived.

Christopher Columbus' First Voyage

Christopher Columbus was a man on a mission. For decades, ever since the Ottoman Turks effectively destroyed the Silk Road, trade ships to the Indies had to sail all the way around Africa. Columbus was convinced there was an easier way to the wealth of Asia. No one had ever dared sail west from Spain before, but he was sure that if one could sail west far enough, one could go all the way around the world and reach India that way.

He was almost right. There was just one small problem: The Americas were in the way.

On September 6th, 1492, Columbus set sail from the Canary Islands in Spain with three ships, a determined—if pressured—crew, and the blessing of the Spanish Crown. His voyage would last for six weeks before reaching land, and it was a terrible six weeks across the open ocean. His three ships, *La Niña*, *La Pinta*, and *Santa María*—were tossed about on the wide seas, and his crew grew all the more petrified on the journey. Their terror only increased when Columbus noted that the needle of his compass was behaving differently on this strange new ocean as they journeyed west. Failing to point to the

North Star, it was wandering inexplicably towards the west, and the strangeness of its behavior made his crew mad with homesickness and fear. Columbus managed to keep them together by speculating that perhaps the compass did not point towards the North Star at all, but rather towards somewhere on Earth, some mystic and invisible point that was truly north. He wasn't wrong either. Columbus had just discovered magnetic declination, a phenomenon that had been vaguely observed in Europe and China before, but was still not accepted knowledge among most navigators.

Finally, after a month of seeing nothing around them but the yawning distance of the open ocean, the crew spotted land. In the early hours of the morning, a young sailor on *Santa Maria* cried out the words that they had all been waiting for so eagerly. Rushing eagerly to the deck, Columbus promptly claimed that he had seen it first, robbing young Rodrigo de Triana of the handsome monetary reward promised to whoever spotted land first on this voyage, and then beheld the island that was the first piece of the Americas to be seen by European eyes: San Salvador. It's uncertain whether Columbus' San Salvador is the same island as which is so named today, but it was certainly in the Turks or Bahamas somewhere, and he was certainly delighted to see it.

Columbus Arrives in Cuba

After spending a few weeks in the Bahamas, Columbus—still looking for India—sailed even further west. And on the 28th of October, 1492, he stumbled upon a land that struck him as spectacularly beautiful even compared to the stunning islands he had just left. Landing on the eastern shore of this new country, he had to question himself momentarily: did he remember India as being quite this beautiful?

Columbus shook off his doubt quickly, however. He decided that this had to be a peninsula of Asia and concluded that his voyage had been successful. This is how the natives who rushed to meet these strange new people earned the name of "Indians," despite actually being among the first and oldest Americans. They were the only "Indians" that Columbus would meet on his voyages west. He never did find that route to India. Instead, he had discovered an island that would later become a priceless treasure in the Spanish Crown, then a thorn in their side, and finally a wildly independent nation that did not allow the world to dictate its actions. He had found Cuba.

The Spaniards and the Natives

At the time of Columbus' arrival in Cuba, the Taíno inhabitants of the island numbered about 350,000. Not knowing what these Spaniards meant for their fates, the natives welcomed them with open arms. Why should they not? They believed that these new people were servants of Yucajú and that they had nothing to fear. Rowing out to the ships in their canoes, the Taíno immediately began a rudimentary form of trade, bringing the hungry Spaniards samples of their crops and other food in exchange for pretty trinkets like glass beads. This is how Europe became acquainted with many of its favorite products of today, including turkey, tobacco, and pineapples. The natives also—willingly or unwillingly—brought Columbus something that he definitely recognized: gold.

The Taíno had been using gold nuggets from the rivers of Cuba and other islands to make jewelry for centuries. Columbus was astounded to see golden rings in the men's ears and golden pendants hanging on the throats of the women, and he promptly stole some of it to take back to Spain. Gold was not the only thing he took. Although violence between the Spaniards and the Taíno was rare during the first voyage, he did succeed in kidnapping a few natives to bring back to Spain as a kind of souvenir.

Columbus and his men spent several weeks resting and relaxing in Cuba, maintaining good relations with the Taíno and learning more about their culture—facts that would be seemingly conveniently forgotten later on, when the Taíno were decreed to be little more than animals. After sailing to Hispaniola (modern Haiti), Columbus was satisfied that he had discovered his route to India. In January 1493, he loaded his sailor's back up and headed home for Spain.

His return to Spain was not uneventful. The *Santa María* had run aground near Hispaniola, so he returned with only the two smaller caravels, although he was able to rescue his sailors. A terrible storm descended upon them during their journey back to Europe. This storm would later turn out to have claimed one hundred other similar caravels from Castilian Spain, but *La Niña* and *La Pinta* made it through, finally reaching Spain in March 1493. Columbus was welcomed like a returning hero.

He wouldn't stay long, however. On September 24th, 1493, Columbus left for "Asia" once again to further explore it and establish a trade route, this time with seventeen ships instead of three. Reassured by the discovery, ship owners and crew members were far more enthusiastic about joining Columbus, and they set forth in a fairly large fleet from Cádiz with high hopes. On April 30th, he returned to Cuba and explored its southern coast. And this was where the trouble began.

Queen Isabella and her husband Ferdinand had ordered Columbus to be friendly to the natives. He thoroughly disobeyed. Desperate to pay back those who had invested in his later voyages, Columbus realized that the quickest way to make money from his voyages would be to trade something immediately valuable. Struggling to find enough gold, he turned to the next available commodity that was familiar to Europeans: slaves. And so, the long history of Cuban slavery began even before anyone knew what Cuba actually was.

560 slaves from various Caribbean islands were shipped back to Spain. Only 360 made it there, the rest exterminated by disease. Sadly, this was only the beginning of the story of how Europeans were to abuse, exploit, and destroy the Taíno people.

In May 1493, before Columbus sailed to Cuba for the second time, Pope Alexander VI issued a papal bull—an edict issued by the Pope—commanding the Spanish to colonize the islands they had discovered, conquer its people, and converts them to Catholicism. The sailors that had visited Cuba in 1492 returned in 1493 not as explorers but as conquistadors, or conquerors. And conquering was exactly what they set out to do.

The friendly Taíno, who had been so free and generous with their resources, were horrified when Columbus began to take groups of them captive for slavery. It was this kidnapping that led to the first armed conflict between the Spanish and Taíno, and like most of the fighting over the next two decades, it was a one-sided contest. The Taíno were well versed in growing food, playing ball games, and consulting with their spirits. They were not adept at warfare. Their wooden weapons were pathetic defenses against the gunpowder and strategy of the Spanish, and their clashes with the invaders were not so much battles as they were complete massacres.

Matters did not improve for the Taíno as the Spanish continued to explore and settle in the New World. In 1509, a sailor named Sebastían de Ocampo was authorized by the governor of Hispaniola to sail around Cuba—then known as Juana—to establish whether it was a peninsula of China as Columbus had expected. In eight months, and sailing against the Gulf Stream, Ocampo circumnavigated the island. The Spanish Crown decided it was time to colonize it in 1511 and sent Diego Velázquez de Cuèllar and his men to conquer the island.

Illustration 1: Monument to Hatuey in Baracoa

Cuba's First National Hero

Velázquez journeyed from Hispaniola to Cuba with a troop of men, bent on conquering the wills of the natives and the landscape of the island. But Hatuey got there first.

Hatuey was a Taíno cacique originally from Hispaniola. When he saw the abominable treatment that the Spaniards inflicted upon the Indians in his home island, he knew two things: Hispaniola was a lost cause, and Cuba had to be warned. Piling into dugout canoes with four hundred of his fellow Taíno, Hatuey traveled to Cuba in an attempt to unify the hundreds of thousands of resident Taíno and defend themselves against the Spanish.

On his arrival in Cuba, Hatuey gathered as many people as he could and delivered a rousing speech. He lifted up a basket filled with priceless treasures, precious stones and glittering gold, and spoke with the authority of a cacique. The Taíno believed that the Spanish served the God they professed to serve—a God of peace, love, and equality. But Hatuey had seen through their hypocrisy and discovered the bitter truth: that they served this loving God about as much as the Pharisees of ancient times had—in name alone. "Here is the God the Spaniards worship," he cried, gesturing to the basket of jewels. "For these they fight and kill; for these they persecute us and that is why we have to throw them into the sea."

He spoke of the many ways in which the Spanish had already begun to abuse the Taíno: their harsh enslavement, their theft of Taíno lands and possessions, their rape of young Taíno women. His speech was rousing, his words were true, and the Cubans did not believe him. These gentle people could not comprehend that the new people they had befriended would treat them so cruelly, and for the most part, they dismissed Hatuey's claims.

Only a handful of Cuban caciques agreed to join Hatuey in resisting the Spaniards. Thus, fleeing into the mountains, Hatuey became the first hero of guerrilla warfare in the history of Cuba—a tradition that would be continued for hundreds of years by resistance and freedom fighters.

When Velázquez arrived to establish a settlement in Baracoa, he was greeted with little resistance from the majority of the Cubans, but Hatuey was ready for him. Coming out of nowhere, his fierce bands of guerrilla warriors attacked the soldiers with devastating speed and surprise. Despite the fact that their wooden weaponry had to be used against Spanish armor ("Incapable of matching us in valor, these cowards cover themselves with iron that our weapons cannot break," Hatuey had said in his speech), the Cuban attacks were strong enough to force the Spanish onto the defensive. Hardly leaving their fort for three months, Velázquez and his men were harried and pushed back by Hatuey's tiny band of determined men.

And the men had every reason to be furious. The Spanish were not merely conquering the Taíno and taking their land. They were actively persecuting and savagely attacking them, often with no provocation and no reason. Historian and clergyman Bartolomé de las Casas recorded, with deep horror, multiple massacres of innocent Taíno. Most notably was an attack on a group of peaceful men, women, and children near Camagüey. Somewhere between 250,000 to 300,000 people journeyed to welcome the Spanish who landed there, preparing a tremendous feast of bread and fish for them. The Spanish enjoyed the feast and then promptly drew their swords and butchered every last one of the unarmed natives. "Their blood ran like a river," las Casas wrote.

This massive slaughter drove Hatuey and his men into open war. Despite their small numbers, Hatuey's army was passionate and driven enough to keep the Spanish back. But Velázquez would not have his prize snatched from him. Terrifying the natives with large mastiffs—creatures that they had never seen before—and capturing some of the fighters to torture until they told him everything, Velázquez captured Hatuey on February 2nd, 1512. He dragged him to a place called Yara, tied him to a stake, and burned him alive.

The resistance died with Hatuey. The Spanish freely murdered thousands of Taíno, sometimes in one-sided battles, sometimes by enslaving them and then proceeding to beat and starve them to death in their mines. But ultimately it was not Spanish swords that would wipe out the Taíno race. It was due to the diseases the Spanish brought with them and for which the Taíno had no natural immunity: most notably smallpox and measles. They died in the thousands, and in less than half a century, a race that had been hundreds of thousands strong was simply wiped out in one of the quickest and most disgusting genocides in history up to that point.

Today, little remains of the Taíno except for fragments of their language found in so many English words today, words like "tobacco" and "hurricane," and in almost every Cuban place name. Bits of their culture have also been absorbed into the modern way of life around the world, most specifically the cultivation of tobacco. It was the Taíno who showed the Spaniards how to grow this plant and then process and smoke it as cigars.

Some Taíno descendants do survive, however. While they were fully conquered in 1514, a few hundred remained alive, pushed into reservations or working as slaves. In 1552, under Spanish New Laws (laws specifically passed to protect the rights of Native Americans in Spanish colonies), the last remaining Cubans were given small towns to live in. Many Spanish men had married Taíno women, and so a large proportion of Cuba's mixed-race populations have scraps of Taíno DNA. But as a culture and as a people, the Taíno were gone by 1550.

Cuba Under Spanish Control

In 1514, Cuba was officially a Spanish colony. Velázquez was named its first governor, and he established multiple settlements, including Baracoa, Santiago de Cuba, and even San Cristóbal de la Habana—a settlement that would develop into modern-day Havana. The Spanish community grew and even began to prosper throughout Cuba, exploring its jungles and starting to grow fields of crops such as corn, tobacco, and sugar. Trade began to blossom between the Old World and the New World, and Cuba would prove instrumental in facilitating this.

But prosperity came at a price. And Africa would pay that price.

Chapter 3 – Slavery and Sugarcane

With the natives all but destroyed, the Spanish set about turning Cuba into their most important settlement in the New World. The Spanish believed that Cuba was rich in gold, and so the colonists transferred their focus from Hispaniola to Cuba. Starting with Ocampo's voyage and continuing with Velázquez's conquest, they began to delve into the island's rich resources.

While gold turned out not to be as abundant as the Spanish had hoped, there were other treasures to be found in Cuba. The most important were tobacco and sugar. Tobacco had been completely alien to Europeans up until Columbus' arrival in the Americas. The plant is native to South and Central America and had been used by the various native peoples for centuries as a kind of cure-all as well as for smoking. The Taíno introduced the Spaniards to smoking the leaves in a crude cigar, and the strange habit spread like wildfire. While some tobacco was taken back to Europe to be cultivated there, it grew best in its place of origin, and soon the Caribbean islands were being called upon to feed the brand-new—and insatiable—European craving.

Sugar, on the other hand, had been well known to the European palate since the Crusades. It was a high-profit luxury, so much so that merchants called it "white gold" and the ordinary citizen could by no means afford this decadent treat. It is thought that Columbus brought sugarcane to the Caribbean during his second voyage in 1493, where the plant absolutely thrived in the climate.

With trade bustling in the island and the rest of the Caribbean, the Spanish were desperate for labor to work in the gold mines, on the ranches, and on tobacco and sugar plantations. As the Taíno died in the thousands, all but wiped out by European diseases, the Spanish began to seek other slaves to fuel this tremendous money-making machine they had stumbled upon. And so less than two decades after Cuba was conquered, the first shipment of African slaves crossed the Atlantic and started the most widespread and brutal era of slavery in the history of the human race.

Timeline of Cuban Slavery

The first slave ship landed in Cuba in 1526. While the slave trade would reach its peak during the eighteenth century, it remained a steady trade throughout the 1500s and 1600s. After the Siege of Havana in 1762, Britain briefly occupied the port and imported Cuba's first large load of slaves—over four thousand in a single year. This boosted the slave trade to the extent that by the 1780s almost twenty thousand slaves were being brought to Cuba in a single decade. In the fifteen years that followed, more than ninety thousand slaves passed through Havana.

Slavery would continue for more than three hundred years until it was finally abolished in the late nineteenth century. In total, about 370,000 slaves would arrive in Cuba—more than the entire Taíno population of the island had been at its peak.

Capturing African Slaves

Strangely enough, slavery was not an entirely unheard of concept in Africa. It was used as a punishment in many countries, similar to how imprisonment is used in the modern world. Others were taken as slaves in order to pay off debts. Chattel slavery, however—the form of slavery in which people are traded as property and owned for their entire lives, with little or no hope of being made free—was hardly practiced at all. At least, not until the slave trade began.

At first, Taíno people were used, but they were soon all but eradicated by disease and overwork. As early as the year 900, Africans were already engaging in slave trade with Arabs. But it was only when the Atlantic slave trade began in earnest that large numbers were being sold into slavery. As native slaves died in the thousands, the Spanish colonizing Cuba turned to another source of "replaceable" human beings to satisfy their appetite for labor. And Africa had a much greater population.

African rulers and smugglers started their part in the slave trade by kidnapping or using prisoners of war. Dragging the slaves from all over Africa to seaports on its western coast in countries like Sierra Leone, the Congo, Senegal, and Angola, they sold them to European traders who would ship them across the Atlantic to Europe and the New World. The appetite for slaves grew so large that some African nations even began to wage war on one another just for the sake of generating enough prisoners of war to sell into slavery. Thus, the toll that slavery took on the African population does not only include those who were enslaved, but the soldiers that fell in these pointless battles. Entire countries' economies were based upon this revolting trade.

The Middle Passage

Perhaps the most inhumane part of the slaves' experience was being shipped across the Atlantic along the notorious "Middle Passage." This was a part of the triangular route taken by slave traders where Africans were shipped to New World destinations. Slavers would start in Europe and travel to Africa laden with goods, which they would use to trade for slaves before taking the slaves over to the Americas and then returning to Europe.

It is difficult to imagine how the slaves must have felt. Not so long ago, they had been free people. Many of them had families, dreams for the future, jobs, and businesses. They had lived in a continent of vast spaces and wild weather, a place with tremendous landscapes and a stormy sky, and now they found themselves crammed shoulder-to-shoulder with strangers in ships that bucked and toiled on the wild ocean. Shackled and chained, stripped of their families, they lay in the festering darkness, sick and dying, dealing with seasickness and with the resultant vomit that sometimes took days to be cleaned out.

Packed hundreds like sardines, these people who had been free only weeks ago were now chained down to plank beds so hard that they caused open sores, sometimes going down to the bone. There were no toilets or hygienic practices on these ships; the sores would only fester and grow horribly infected. And this was only one of the many horrific trials that the slaves had to endure on the ships.

Like the Taíno, the Africans had no resistance to European diseases like measles, smallpox, and dysentery. In the filthy, stifling environment of the slave ships, crammed in as tightly as they were, disease spread like wildfire. Slaves died in the hundreds and sometimes were left in the hold for days, often chained to living slaves, before their bodies were thrown carelessly overboard. Food and water were extremely limited, as was space. However, in order to make the slaves at least somewhat useful on arrival in the New World, slave ship crews would drive them onto the deck and force them to dance for exercise.

This was the one opportunity that slaves had to rebel, and rebel they did, sometimes with disastrous consequences. There were many uprisings on those dread seas, and most of them ended badly for the slaves. Hundreds were killed in rebellions; others, seeing that the fight was fruitless, chose to throw themselves overboard instead, dying in the shark-infested waters. Slave suicides became so prevalent that ships were equipped with nets to make it harder for slaves to kill themselves. Others chose a more passive form of suicide by refusing food and water. Despite efforts by crews to force-feed their "merchandise," many slaves died like this as well.

Crews also didn't have a good time on slave ships. Most hated the trade and refused to willingly accept work on a slave ship, so many were coerced or kidnapped. After delivering slaves to the Caribbean, the ship needed much less crew, so crew members were starved or beaten in an attempt to either kill them or force them to jump ship in the Caribbean. About one in every five crewmen on the slave ships died.

Slave mortality rates were even worse. William Wilberforce, an advocate for the abolition of the slave trade in the eighteenth century, quoted the number as being about 12.5 percent, or one in every eight slaves. Mortally sick slaves were often thrown overboard while they were still living, and there was basically no provision for medicine or healthcare of any kind.

Arriving in the New World

Those slaves that survived the trip to the New World were weak and sickly on arrival. Slavers needed to sell them as quickly as possible in order to turn a profit and return to Europe for another load, so no time was given for them to recuperate from their harsh journey. Driven into pens like cattle, the slaves were washed, rubbed with palm oil to hide some of their wounds, and given rudimentary clothes. The mortality rate was still fairly high—about four and a half percent of slaves still died before they were sold on to their new owners.

Slaves destined for Cuba were primarily taken to Havana, although other ports were also used. Once they had been cleaned up for sale, the most popular method of selling slaves was known as the "scramble." This was a horrifying experience for the Africans. They were at this point incapable of understanding the Europeans as they didn't speak Spanish or English; they had no way of knowing what was happening as they were herded into a pen. The crack of a gunshot—likely the first gunshot some of them had ever heard—

signaled slave buyers to rush into the pen and seize whichever slaves appealed to them. Rumors that these strange white men had captured them in order to eat them must never have looked as likely as at that moment, with greedy, hungry plantation owners rushing upon the terrified slaves.

This was also the point at which most families were separated forever. Those who had made friends during the six-week voyage from Africa were now stripped of those as well; children were torn away from their mothers, couples ripped apart, families destroyed as new owners carried them off. They had no say in their fate. It was obey or die, and though many chose to die, enough of their spirits had been broken that the trade remained lucrative for slave captains and plantation owners everywhere.

Life in the Plantations

When a slave first set foot in sugar plantation, their life expectancy immediately dropped due to the harsh nature of the work, abuse by owners and overseers, and appalling living conditions, most slaves were not expected to live for longer than eight years on a plantation. Owners had little reason to attempt to extend this life expectancy; with the abundance of slaves coming in through Havana, it was cheaper and easier just to buy new ones.

For modern First World minds, it's difficult to comprehend the suffering that these sugar slaves went through. If you were a slave, you worked for sixteen to twenty hours a day; that means that you only slept for as little as three hours—less than half the amount of sleep that normal adults need, never mind those hours engaged in so many hours of hard physical labor. The work was backbreaking, causing your muscles to ache as your eyes burned with sleep deprivation. The tropical sun beat down on you as you worked in the open cane fields with little protection. And if you're weary limbs slowed, or you paused even for a moment, or stumbled onto the hot, rich earth for a moment's respite, the overseer's whip would sing through the air and crack down on your back and limbs, leaving open wounds that stung with the sweat that was rolling into them from your toiling muscles. You worked until you dropped, and if you dropped, you were beaten. And all the time as you worked, you were producing a luxury for a spoiled and privileged few, a mere tasty morsel that had little real value beyond pleasure.

You lived in a stifling, airless enclosure known as a barracoon, which had no hygiene or separate toilet area and little comfort. If you were a woman, you ran the risk of being raped by your masters, or if you bore children to a fellow slave, you could be beaten until you miscarried or have your children stripped away from you and sold as soon as possible.

If you were like many of the slaves, you tried to think of ways to rebel. Perhaps you considered suicide, the most final and most silent rebellion that the slaves could think of, the one thing that the overseers failed to deny them. Many slaves chose to hang themselves from trees, preferring death over bondage, believing that their spirits would fly back to Africa and be free once again. Their bodies, however, remained in Cuba, where owners would cut off their hands and heads and display them for all the other slaves to see in an attempt to dishearten them.

Some slaves tried to rebel more actively by causing uprisings, which were common throughout the sugarcane plantations. Unbeknownst to many slaves, as the 19th century approached, blacks outnumbered white and mulatto (mixed race) Cubans, so the fear of a rebellion was very real—a fear that only intensified after the 1791 Haitian Revolution during which an entire nation of slaves threw off their bonds and turned on their owners, driving them out to the sea.

But the Cuban slaves never staged a united rebellion, and the Haitians' newfound freedom became increased bondage for Africans imported to Cuba. Once leading the sugar exporter of the New World Haiti no longer had slaves to fuel this booming industry, as its newly freed population turned to subsistence farming. The surviving plantation owners fled to Cuba, where the sugar industry boomed, and the number of slaves being imported skyrocketed into the hundreds of thousands.

That left one last route for rebellion, one which many slaves took: escape. They had no means of returning to Africa, but they could try to carve out a secret life of something close to freedom in the mountains of eastern Cuba, and so slave communities began to pop up in Guantanamo and the Sierra Maestra. These were known as *palenques*. Escaped slaves mixed with what was left of the native Cubans, developing little settlements of their own; these people and their descendants were known as maroons.

Ultimately, most slaves were stuck working the cane fields until they died. Causes of death were many—simple exhaustion, dehydration, suicide, or disease. Others were just beaten to death by their owners who used brutal punishments to keep the slaves in line, including putting them into stocks and whipping them until they bled. The Spanish Black Code, a set of laws passed in 1789 that were supposed to protect slaves from abuse, was little help; most slave owners simply disregarded them, and they were seldom enforced.

Twentieth-century Cuban poet Nicolás Guillèn's simplistic poem, "Caña" (Sugarcane), gives a powerful voice to the suffering of Cuban slaves.

The Negro
bound to the canefield.
The Yankee above is canefield.
The earth beneath was canefield.
Blood
seeps out of us!

Chapter 4 – War

Illustration 2: British ships in the Seven Years' War

As more and more treasures of every description were discovered in the Americas and shipped back to the Old World, Cuba's prosperity boomed. Not only did the island produce all manners of useful merchandise, its new capital became one of the main ports used by trade ships traveling to Europe. While Santiago de Cuba was named the first official capital of Cuba, Havana was quickly established as its most important port, and eventually became the capital. Its position on the western coast of the island, as well as its convenient bay, made it a perfect stopover for trade ships headed to the Old World laden with Caribbean and American treasures. Ships stopped at this town to pick up water, meat, leather, timber, tobacco, and sugar; usually by this time they were also laden with merchandise from other countries, especially gold and silver. They used Havana as a final rest stop before beginning the long trek back to Europe.

By the mid-sixteenth century, almost all Spanish trade ships—even those coming from Mexico, Panama, and other Caribbean islands—stopped at Havana. This started to attract the attention of those who wanted the blossoming town for themselves, those who wanted to invade it and plunder its bounty. Cuba was being put on the map as a desirable haven of treasure and trade, and the world had taken notice. For the first time since Spanish colonization, the island was under attack from outside forces.

But this was no ordinary war and these were no ordinary soldiers. These were pirates.

The Real Pirates of the Caribbean

Pirates were the bandits of the high seas. Originally, they were groups of rebels who forsook navy or merchant ships in order to do their own thing, living for their own interests and doing as they pleased. The Atlantic was rich with trade ships, most of which were slow, ponderous, and poorly defended, making them the perfect targets for swift and savage pirate fleets that would descend upon them and pillage their holds for treasure, often massacring the crews.

Pirates themselves often did not live for very long; their lives were risky, but many considered the freedom and comparative luxury of the pirate life to be worth the risk. Escaped slaves also often joined pirates in exchange for their freedom and for vengeance on those same traders who had taken them away from everything they had once loved.

The pirate era lasted for centuries. It began in the early 1500s, peaking during the Golden Age of Piracy from the mid-1600s to the early 1700s and only diminishing when European countries united in defense against the remaining pirates in the nineteenth century. During the Golden Age, whole ports consisted entirely of pirate communities, such as Port Royal in Jamaica and Nassau in the Bahamas.

As pirates gained strength, some countries decided to take advantage of this new method of acquiring wealth by hiring pirates known as privateers to attack ships belonging to enemy countries. Privateers would then bring the treasure back to their employers and split the profits. This helped to fund the wars that were cropping up all over Europe during this era.

The Spanish Treasure Fleet and Sacking of Havana

Spain continued to send ships loaded with silver from the Americas to the Old World, but individual ships were often not defended at all and proved to be easy pickings for pirates. Faced by this tremendous financial loss, the Spanish Crown had to come up with a solution. The idea they settled on was the Spanish Treasure Fleet.

Instead of sailing to Europe one by one, Spanish merchant ships were now compelled to go in a group. Two fleets would set sail from Europe each year, one departing for Mexico in the spring, another heading to Colombia and Panama in August. They would then spend the winter in the Americas loading up with merchandise before meeting at Havana for the journey home the next spring. They would be flanked and protected by the formidable Spanish Armada, a fleet of warships that daunted even the most reckless of pirates.

Havana itself still remained a target that pirates could not resist. It was attacked repeatedly by a variety of pirates, the most notable attack being performed by Jacques de Sores. This French corsair had earned his nickname of "The Avenging Angel" by being an exceptionally ruthless and terrifying pirate. Most pirates killed in order to gain wealth; the Avenging Angel sometimes killed just for the sake of shedding blood. This apparent psychopath considered Havana a haven of treasure, and in 1555, he decided it was time that treasure became his. His four ships attacked the town late at night, his pirates disembarking to pillage and lay waste to Havana. Unfortunately for de Sores, there was no real wealth to be found in the town; it all passed through the treasure ships instead of remaining in Havana. An enraged de Sores burned Havana to the ground, hanged many of its residents, and finally left it in ruins.

Spanish authorities responded by fortifying their precious harbor, building two fortresses, "El Morro" and "La Punta," at the channel of the bay. For more about the sacking of Havana and about its fortifications, see *A History of Havana: A Captivating Guide to the History of the Capital of Cuba from Christopher Columbus' Arrival to Fidel Castro.*

The Sacking of Santiago de Cuba

De Sores was not the only terrifying corsair to pillage Cuba's coastline. In fact, he was an associate of an even more famous and bloodthirsty pirate: François le Clerc. Le Clerc was a famously reckless pirate whose specialty was boarding beleaguered ships ahead of his men, a wild tactic that eventually almost killed him, as he lost a leg and severely injured an arm in a battle with an English ship. This did not slow him down for long. As soon as the stump was healed, le Clerc strapped on a peg leg and carried on as if nothing had happened, perhaps with even more gusto than before. This earned him the nickname of "Jambe de Bois," French for "Peg Leg." The modern tradition of peg-legged pirates descends from him.

Le Clerc was in charge of a fleet of ten pirate ships, one of which was commanded by Jacques de Sores, and another by le Clerc himself. This fleet headed for the Caribbean and began to raid the shores of Puerto Rico, Hispaniola, and Cuba, moving relentlessly northward. In 1554, le Clerc would reach Santiago de Cuba, which was then still the capital. Aided by the rest of his fleet, le Clerc took the city with almost no resistance, proceeding to stay there for a solid month as the pirates burned, ransacked, and looted with happy abandon. They stripped Santiago de Cuba of all of its wealth, finally departing with eighty thousand pesos—several thousand U.S. dollars in today's money, not accounting for five hundred years of inflation—and leaving the city practically in ruins. It was le Clerc's attack that was responsible for the Cuban capital officially being made Havana instead; Santiago de Cuba never recovered fully from the sacking.

This hapless city would be sacked twice more: in 1603 and again in 1662. During the Anglo-Spanish War, British privateers wreaked havoc upon Spanish ships and ports alike, and it was natural that they would turn their attention to Cuban ports. Havana's defenses proved to be a strong enough deterrent to keep them at bay, but Santiago de Cuba was not as well defended. At the time, it was still the second-to-largest city in Cuba, and it became Privateer Christopher Cleeve's main target when he set sail from England in February 1603. He reached the Caribbean in April and set his sights on Santiago de Cuba, reaching a nearby bay on May 12th and spending a month plundering the city for all its riches before leaving it in ruins.

When the war ended, the Spanish started construction on a new fortress to protect Santiago de Cuba. The Castillo de San Pedro de la Roca took decades to complete, and was still not finished in 1662 when a band of British freebooters returned to the city. These were led by Christopher Myngs, a notoriously cruel pirate leader who commanded fleets of buccaneers because he gave them free rein to plunder, murder, and rape as they wished. Despite the half-finished fortress, the city was almost completely destroyed. The San Pedro de la Roca Castle was also almost destroyed, but its construction would be restarted and finally finished in 1700. It is now a UNESCO World Heritage Site and a beautifully preserved piece of architecture paying homage to the era when pirates razed entire cities to the ground.

The era was about to come to an end. In the late 18th century, pirates finally became more trouble than they were worth. Even those pirates who worked under the employ of warring countries had a tendency to misbehave; at their very hearts, they were the quintessential rebels, free spirits who couldn't be commanded, and had a savage streak that had no qualms with planting a literal or metaphorical dagger in somebody's back. Various powers started to ban piracy, and with armies gaining strength and no support for piracy, the pirates gradually just faded into near-nonexistence.

The War of Jenkins' Ear

Cuba's troubles were far from over, however. It had suffered the conquest of the Taíno by the Spanish and then the pirate raids along its coast, but now for the first time it was about to be plunged into the chaos of an intercontinental war. This was the uniquely-named War of Jenkins' Ear, a conflict as serious as its name is silly.

It all started with the *Rebecca*, a British brig. She was sailing home from a trade visit to the West Indies, making her way towards Havana for provisions before tackling the journey across the Atlantic to England in April 1731. Her captain, Robert Jenkins, was on deck watching the welcoming arms of Havana Bay draw closer. Due to strained relations between Britain and Spain, he knew that his well-laden ship could only bear her cargo because of *asiento*, the contract that allowed Britain to trade with Spanish colonies, especially in slaves. So, when he saw the Spanish Coast Guard approaching the *Rebecca*, he wasn't very worried.

He should have been. The Coast Guard was led by Juan de León Fandiño, a commander who bordered on privateer. This swashbuckling Spaniard was sick of the British, and he had heard tell that Spain regretted establishing *asiento*, wanting to take its monopoly back from the British. Now he found himself aboard one of those hated ships that were stealing Spain's trade from under its nose. Jenkins had expected a friendly exchange. What he got was effectively torture.

Fandiño's men attacked Jenkins' unprepared crew. Savagely, they rushed through the hold of the *Rebecca*, plundering her of all her bounty, including Jenkins' instruments for navigation. They detained the crew as prisoners for an entire day, starving and mocking them as they stripped the *Rebecca*'s wealth from her. Finally, as a parting insult before leaving, they pushed Jenkins up against the mast and tied him up. Fandiño drew his flashing cutlass and gave a smile whose sharp curve echoed the shape of the blade. Then he delivered a swift cut to Jenkins' face, slitting his ear. Blood poured down Jenkins' neck and shoulder as the laughing Spaniards closed in, another crew member grasping the severed ear and, with an excruciating twist, yanking it clean off. Fandiño handed Jenkins his ear back and told him to go and show it to his king, telling him, "The same will happen to him." With that, the Spaniards were gone.

Prevented from docking at Havana for supplies, the *Rebecca* was forced to limp half-crippled and plundered back to London. It reached the Thames in June 1731, and days later, Jenkins appeared before Parliament to present his unhappy case to the king. According to some accounts, Jenkins solidified his sad story by producing the remains of his lost ear floating in a jar like a gruesome pickle. This was the last straw that the strained Anglo-Spanish relations needed. By 1739, official war was declared, and so the War of Jenkins' Ear began.

The Invasion of Cuba

The war had been raging for two years, mainly in the West Indies, and Vice Admiral Edward Vernon had just been defeated—again. The British commander had put painstaking efforts into gathering one of the largest fleets ever assembled. At Port Royal, Jamaica, he had put together a force of 27,000 men strong, crammed into 186 ships. With this tremendous army, he set sail on Cartagena de Indias in modern-day Colombia. He was so assured of the victory that before the battle was over, he sent reports of his triumph to Jamaica.

The reports were false. The little garrison of Spaniards at Cartagena hung on to their city just long enough for yellow fever to strike the British. With all those men trapped in the cramped ships, the disease spread like wildfire. By May 9th, 1741, six thousand British men had died, and Vernon was forced to retreat.

With morale and health at a desperate low in his army, Vernon set his sights on an easier target: Cuba. He knew that attacking Havana would be fruitless, but the south and east of the island was sparsely populated and poorly defended.

Vernon and another British commander, Major-General Thomas Wentworth, had only four thousand troops left in fighting form when they landed at Guantanamo Bay on the 4th and 5th of August. The resultant invasion was possibly one of the most slow-paced and lackadaisical in history. The Spanish garrison at La Catalina was a quarter of the size of the British force and fled without resisting them, but the British were already half defeated by the time they landed in Cuba. Yellow fever was still spreading through the troops. Sick, disheartened, and exhausted by their recent defeat, the men limped through the Cuban countryside, occasionally harassed by Spanish guerrillas, failing to achieve anything or capture any major towns. They would continue to stumble aimlessly around the island for four months. By the beginning of December, more than half of the men were sick, and Vernon realized that he had wasted enough time in Cuba. They evacuated on the 9th of December, heading back to Port Royal, beaten even though they had been largely unopposed.

However, the British were not done with Cuba yet. Santiago de Cuba was about to face another attack.

The Battle of Santiago de Cuba

In 1742, shortly after the British retreated from their dismal attempt at invading Cuba, the War of Jenkins' Ear merged into the War of the Austrian Succession. Archduchess Maria Theresia of Austria was poised to inherit her father's many titles. Charles VI had been Holy Roman Emperor, the Archduke of Austria, and the king of Bohemia, Hungary, Serbia, and Croatia; now that he was gone, his strong-willed daughter was ready to step into his shoes, but France, Prussia, and Bavaria would have none of it. These countries protested that a woman could not hold such power. Maria Theresa refused to go down without a fight, and joined by Britain, the Dutch Republic, Sardinia, and Saxony, she fought for her right to hold the titles.

Spain quickly jumped into the fight on France's side, and the messy War of Jenkins' Ear simply melded into the even more widespread conflict that had now engulfed most of Europe. This did not by any means bring peace to the New World, however. The British were still bent on capturing Cuba and other Spanish colonies, and so in 1748, Sir Charles Knowles was sent to attempt the capture of Santiago de Cuba.

A controversial and colorful character, Charles Knowles was born in 1704 and joined the navy when he was only fourteen years old. One of his first roles was as captain's servant aboard the *HMS Lenox*, and he worked his way up the ranks to become governor of Louisbourg by 1746. Both an engineer and a skilled naval commander, Knowles' varied career was about to reach its all-time low as the War of the Austrian Succession began to draw to a close.

Knowles had been commanding the British forces in Jamaica since April 1747, and he launched his first major offensive in February 1748 by capturing Fort Saint Louis de Sud in modern-day Haiti. Bolstered by this victory, he headed for Santiago de Cuba in March, arriving on the coastline on the afternoon of the 28th.

The *HMS Plymouth* was selected to scout out the area before commencing the attack. The elegant ship of the line sailed to the entrance of the city, aided by a Spanish pilot that had been taken prisoner by the British. He was forced, on pain of death, to guide the British attack on his own people. With his assistance, the *Plymouth*'s captain concluded that the attack would not be difficult, and returned to the fleet with confidence. Perhaps with a little too much confidence. They attacked the next morning, led into the harbor by the *Plymouth*, and opened fire on the fortifications with their massive cannons; the *Canterbury* was particularly important here, as she was fitted with a 10" mortar that inflicted devastating damage on the city. As other ships of the line focused on shelling the fortifications, the *Plymouth* sailed closer to the city, ready to bombard it with her sixty guns, but her efforts would be thwarted. With the thunder of the cannons all around him, her captain pushed further into the harbor, propelled by a brisk sea breeze, as directed by the Spanish pilot. They were dangerously close to the city when the captain of the *Plymouth* spotted the threatening shape of a defensive chain strung across the harbor, effectively blocking the *Plymouth* from entering. Trapped between Spanish fortifications, the *Plymouth* was in trouble and her captain knew it. He scrambled to send longboats out to try and clear the chain, but it was too late. The Spanish opened heavy fire on the *Plymouth*, pouring ammunition into her, blowing great splintered holes in her proud curves. The rudder went first; then the mainmast, with a terrible crack, came tumbling down, scattering sailors as it fell. Finally, even her bowsprit was blown completely away, leaving only splintered remnants. The *Plymouth* was utterly disabled. Her few survivors were rescued by another British ship, which towed them back out to the safety of the sea on their half-destroyed ship.

The *Plymouth* was not the only one to take heavy fire. Knowles's precious flagship, the *HMS Cornwall*, had lost most of her stern and also had to be towed to safety. One hundred men were killed, two hundred more wounded, and the beautiful ships all but destroyed. Once again, the British had to leave Santiago de Cuba with their tails between their legs, mostly thanks to poor leadership on Knowles' part.

The war was drawing to a close in Europe. Britain and France had made peace, Silesia had been surrendered, and Maria Theresa was taking her crowns. There was talk of peace between Spain and Britain, although nothing had been finalized. Knowles was facing disgrace at the end of this war and he didn't like it. He had only one chance at redemption now—he had to take some Spanish ships.

The Battle of Havana

Leaving Santiago de Cuba, Knowles knew that the Spanish Treasure Fleet had likely just left Havana to sail back to the Old World. While he had little hope of attacking Havana itself, he knew that it would be a feather in his cap if he could capture one of those treasure-laden

Spanish ships. Setting a course to intercept the fleet, he met up with Captain Charles Holmes on September 30th aboard the *HMS Lenox*—the very ship on which his navy career had started. Holmes had recently sighted a Spanish fleet, and the two captains agreed to launch a privateer-style attack together.

Meanwhile, Admiral Andrès Reggio of the Havana Squadron was patrolling Spain's shipping lanes to protect them from just such an attack. Reggio had been in Havana for nine years improving her fortifications, but with no real attack having ever been launched on the city during this war, perhaps he had grown a little complacent. At any rate, when the British fleet sighted his squadron on October 11th, 1748, they were a disorganized mass and utterly unprepared for any real fighting. In fact, when Reggio sighted the British ships, he thought they were Spanish trade ships and set a course directly for them in an attempt to protect them.

The British could not believe their luck. Their enemies were coming straight into their laps. Knowles was able to gain the weather gauge—the advantageous upwind position for battle—and by that afternoon. The *Canterbury* and the *Warwick* were within range of the Spanish. The peaceful ocean erupted into a chaos of cannon fire. The air was filled with smoke, spray, and splinters as the ships bombarded each other with devastating consequences. The newly-repaired *Cornwall* and the *Lenox* were slow to come to the other ships' aid, only getting into the fight more than an hour later when they launched an attack on the Spanish *Conquistador*. Two of its masts were blown to smithereens, leaving the ship almost incapable of maneuvering. This left it completely vulnerable to attack, and the *HMS Strafford* took advantage of its weakness and attacked it broadside, pouring a devastating number of cannonballs into its heart. Soon its commanders were dead, and the *Conquistador* had to surrender.

The Spanish flagships, *Africa* and *Invencible*, were also in deep trouble. With the *Conquistador* captured, *Strafford* and *Canterbury* launched an attack on the *Africa*, and two other ships pursued the

Invencible until it was silenced, its guns disabled. The *Invencible* escaped; the *Africa* was not so lucky. Her masts were utterly destroyed, leaving her completely helpless and so badly damaged that Reggio and her crew could only just steer her into a little bay east of Havana, where they fled the ship and blew her up to prevent the British from capturing her.

By nightfall, the squadron was scattered; the *Invencible* limping away with almost no defenses, the *Conquistador* defeated, the *Africa* a fireball reflected in the shimmering ocean as her smoke rose into the starry sky. Knowles was in the ideal position to press home his advantage, capture more ships, and maybe even attack Havana itself. It's unclear why exactly he failed to do so, allowing most of the squadron to get away. Perhaps he felt he had proven himself enough; perhaps he finally realized that this action was pointless in the face of looming peace. It's neither reasoning sat well with Knowles' commanders.

The next morning, a Spanish sloop intercepted the triumphant British with the news that a treaty had been signed between Britain and Spain. Knowles dropped off his prisoners in Cuba, but they kept the *Conquistador*, towing their sorry prize back to Port Royal. Knowles' commanders were not impressed. He would later face a court-martial for his failure to take Santiago de Cuba and to win a more decisive victory in the Battle of Havana. He was reprimanded for his poor tactics, as was Reggio, who was accused of being disorganized when the British came across his squadron.

The Seven Years' War

After decades of unease and almost ten years of war, Europe finally settled into a tense semblance of peace, but it would not last long. The continent had been involved in various wars for more than a century, and the problem would only get worse before it could get better. It finally erupted into the largest conflict the world had ever seen in 1756. This war is properly known as the Seven Years' War, but it has since been referred to as World War Zero for its sheer scale and the involvement of almost every major power in the world at the time. Cuba was largely left alone except for the jewel in its crown, Havana, which was besieged and captured by the British in 1762. After the war ended, it was returned to Spanish control in exchange for the whole of Florida, and the brief British occupation turned out to be advantageous to the economy of the city and the country as trade was opened up. The Seven Years' War and the Siege of Havana are described in more detail in *History of Havana: A Captivating Guide to the History of the Capital of Cuba from Christopher Columbus' Arrival to Fidel Castro.*

Chapter 5 – The Cry of Yara

David Turnbull had hated Havana, but this was so much worse.

The Scotsman had traveled all over the world since being made a foreign correspondent for *The Times* in London. He had seen Paris and Brussels, Madrid and the Hague, and had now been in Cuba for a few years, having been named the British consul there. Stationed in the capital, Turnbull had spent much of his time wandering through the slave markets and prisons, questioning slave owners and trying to expose the horrors of the trade. He believed in abolition with a fiery determination that had led him halfway across the world to a country where slavery was still legal, and what he found there had disgusted him. Barracoons filled with bewildered teenagers fresh from Africa. Slaves were being tied to whipping posts and lashed until they bled for the tiniest transgression. And if there were no transgressions, sometimes slaves would be whipped anyway, just to "maintain their master's authority."

It all had sickened him, but nothing had prepared him for the sugar plantations. He had never witnessed such mistreatment before, not even on the British plantations. The stifling barracoons the ridiculous hours, the unrelenting whipping, the ceaseless cruelty

It all fueled the fire, and he knew he had to do something about the trade. He had to get the Spanish to let go of their death grip on the slave trade.

La Escalera

David Turnbull was made the British consul in 1840, but he only lasted in Cuba for two years before Spanish authorities discovered that he was stirring up a slave revolt and booted him out of the country. Still, the seeds of rebellion had been planted, and Cuba was fertile soil.

Not only was Spain one of the last empires to cling to the slave trade, but Cubans themselves were getting restless with Spanish control. Their country was prospering, and the world was waking up to the horrors of slavery, causing Cuban citizens to start to reject the trade too. The colonial government oppressed all Cuban-born citizens, and most of Cuba's prosperity was going directly back to Spain; one-tenth of the population was gaining nine-tenths of the country's wealth. Even Cubans born of Spanish descent were feeling the pinch. Essentially, the conflict arose between Spanish-born people who had immigrated to Cuba, and everyone who had been born in Cuba and slaves.

Cuba had been restless for decades. The first real uprising of 1826 opened Spanish eyes to the real unhappiness that was brewing, and to the fact that it was not only slaves who wanted to throw off their chains. Andrés Manuel Sánchez was a mulatto, but the other leader of the uprising, Francisco de Agüero, was as white as the Spaniards. They both were executed and the uprising was crushed before it could go beyond the planning stages, but it made one truth evident: slaves and free people alike were tired of Spanish control. Rebellion was brewing, and the Spanish Crown was terrified of it, knowing that with blacks, mulattos, and even white Cubans joining forces, the Spanish could be outnumbered. So, in 1843 and 1844, they cracked down—hard.

Small uprisings had been taking place all around the island starting in March of 1843, most notably on the sugar plantations. Restless slaves rose up against their masters, overwhelming their overseers by the sheer force of numbers, and charged unarmed against those who would oppose them; some were aided by free people, which made them even more powerful. These uprisings were stopped in their tracks, but the regularity with which they popped up made the Spanish authorities take notice. They arrested rebelling slaves, witnesses, and other suspects, and then tortured them for information. This is how the conspiracy they uncovered was named: by their method of torture. Suspects were pushed up against a ladder, bound to it, and then whipped until they either confessed or told whatever lie the Spanish wanted to hear. The conspiracy was named La Escalera: "the ladder."

David Turnbull was already safely back in Britain when the Spanish accused him of being the leader of the conspiracy and escaped any real consequences. But the slaves on the plantations suffered so much that 1844 was called the Year of the Lash. Terrified slave owners treated their slaves more harshly than ever. White abolitionists were viewed with fear and suspicion; free people of color, already oppressed under the current social structure, were even more so. Spanish tyranny was destroying lives, and it had to be ended.

But it was not a slave or even an abolitionist who would begin Cuba's long and harsh struggle for independence. It was a plantation owner.

Francisco Vicente Aguilera was the wealthiest man in eastern Cuba, owning hundreds of acres of fertile land, canefields, livestock, and, of course, slaves. Aguilera quickly became known for never purchasing a slave in his life; the slaves he had were all those he had inherited from his father, and unbeknownst to them, they would soon be set free. Aguilera was planning a rebellion. He used his influence secretly throughout his circles, persuading other powerful men, mostly plantation owners, to join his conspiracy to revolt against the Spanish.

One of these men, and one who would become the face of the revolution, was a plantation owner and lawyer named Carlos Manuel de Céspedes.

The Cry of Yara

It was a balmy morning in the tropical Cuban autumn, and the slaves of Le Damajagua stood patiently in their barracoon, waiting for the bell to ring and drag them back to work in the sugar mill. Although working here had not been so bad lately; there was little whipping, good food, and unexpected kindness. They had even begun to hear the rumors of freedom that had been flying around the island, although many of them were more concerned about the stories of uprisings that were violently and horribly crushed. Some of the slaves still remembered stories of the Year of the Lash twenty-four years ago. Few of them had actually experienced it—sugar slaves didn't live long enough for that—but the terror of it still resonated with them.

At last, the bell rang. The slaves filed meekly out of their barracoon and headed up to the front of the sugar mill, blinking in the sharp sunlight. Their master, Céspedes, was waiting on the steps of the sugar mill. The air was charged with excitement, and the slaves shuffled hesitantly into their places, glancing at the sheet of paper that had been nailed to the door of the mill. People they didn't know were gathered around and a flag they didn't recognize had been hoisted above the mill. What was happening?

The slaves stared up at their master, waiting for him to give them their orders. Some guessed at what was happening and trembled with hope; others, with fear. Céspedes smiled broadly at them, obviously excited. His next words cut straight to the slaves' hearts.

He was setting them all free. They were all free.

The slaves broke down into jubilation, into crying, into stunned shock at this news. Riding the wave of emotion, Céspedes proclaimed his manifesto, which had been signed by him and fifteen other independence fighters. The manifesto spoke of freedom and equality; it sought complete abolition of slavery and a just constitution that would grant rights to all Cubans, no matter their heritage or birthplace. Céspedes rallied other plantation owners and their slaves to fight alongside him, and borne on a heady tide of hope, they marched on nearby Yara on October 11th, 1868.

The Ten Years' War Begins

The war began, and almost ended, with Yara. The small town slipped through the small rebel force's fingers, and the Spanish relaxed slightly, thinking that the rebellion had been crushed as easily as those before it. But it was not to be. Losing no momentum, the rebels set their sights on Bayamo, a bigger and far more important city. By October 14th, Bayamo had fallen, and the rebels had taken control over it. Cuba's current national anthem, *La Bayamesa*, was penned at Bayamo after this victory.

With Bayamo in rebel hands, the Spanish army was forced to take them seriously. Even more so when city after city in the Oriente Province began to join the rebellion, revolting against their Spanish inhabitants and rising in arms against their oppressors. First came Camagüey in November 1868, then Las Villas in February 1869. Even though the western regions such as Havana did not join the revolution, it spread like wildfire through the east, and the rebel movement began to gain strength and numbers at a speed that terrified the Spanish army. They made some attempts to negotiate with the rebels, but these were all in vain. In 1869, they began to wage an open war that was not so much focused on victory as it was on extermination. There were no fair trials and no quarter was given. Rebels were executed immediately if arrested, ships caught carrying weapons—usually from other rebels and exiles in the United States—had all their passengers murdered at once, and strict curfews were put in place, always enforced by death. Women and children were sent to brutal concentration camps in the thousands. The Spanish were looking for reasons to kill, but far from frightening the insurgents into silence, their new policies were only fuel for the fire.

By April 1869, the movement had grown to the extent that a meeting was held in Camagüey to organize its army and government more efficiently. Céspedes was elected as its leader, the first president of the Cuban Republic in Arms, and Manuel de Quesada was the chief of Armed Forces. Led by these men, the guerrilla war began in earnest. Armed with machetes, horses, some firearms, and the determination of men who wanted freedom or death, the independence fighters became known as the Mambises, named for a black Spanish soldier who defected to the rebel side during the Dominican Republic's struggle for independence. Originally the term was a racial slur, but the fighters adopted it and wore it with pride.

As the war continued, the rebels gained strength. By the peak of the fighting in 1872, there were about 40,000 rebels in the force. They were underfed and poorly armed, but they continued their struggle against the Spanish Army despite horrendous atrocities committed by Spain. As well as the endless killing in the war, innocents were murdered without cause, usually by the two sets of Voluntary Corps; one example would be the horrific massacre of eight university students in Havana. The students had had no part in the uprising, but were killed as a way for the Spanish to show their ruthlessness and authority.

The Death of Céspedes

Céspedes remained the figurehead of the war until 1872, when Ignacio Agramonte, one of their most important generals, was killed in battle. In the rising pressure of the war, trouble was brewing within the Republic in Arms too. This finally culminated in personal and political fallout regarding their constitution, which ultimately resulted in Céspedes being deposed.

Far from being discouraged by how he had been treated, Céspedes decided that he could help Cuba better using another tactic: traveling to the United States to source more weaponry and men to send to Cuba. The Republic denied him permission, leaving him trapped in a country where he no longer had any allies. Hiding in a mountain refuge, he only had one escort to protect him, and it wasn't enough. By February 1874, Céspedes was dead, killed by Spanish troops.

It would seem that deposing him was a mistake on the part of the rebel government because the war was all downhill from there. After his death, the war was confined to the eastern provinces where it had begun and began to peter out as the superior Spanish resources wore the Mambises out. When the Third Carlist War in Spain ended in 1876, 250,000 troops were sent to Cuba, and the rebellion was effectively over. The government was dissolved in 1878, and the Pact of Zanjón was signed, concluding the war. The Pact was little consolation for the rebels. It made few concessions, liberating only those slaves who had fought in the war, granting no steps towards independence, and reestablishing Spain's iron grip on the island.

Most of the Mambises fled in exile to the United States, but they weren't finished yet. Another uprising was being planned.

The Little War

One of these rebel leaders was Calixto Garcia. He was just a teenager when he joined the uprising that blossomed into the Ten Years' War, and by the time it ended, he was second-in-command of the rebel army. Fleeing to New York City after the Pact of Zanjón, Garcia wasn't done with independence yet.

In August 1879, eighteen months after the Ten Years' War ended, Garcia returned to Cuba. Gathering a handful of revolutionaries, he launched another uprising, but this one fell very flat very fast. The people were sick of fighting; many concluded that even oppression was better than war, and few joined the struggle. Resources were also at an all-time low on an island that had been so depleted by a decade of war. The Little War was a sad struggle that was ended almost before it begun. One by one, the hopeful rebels had to surrender, until they were all defeated by September 1880.

Abolition at Last

Although independence seemed out of the question after the terrible defeat of the Little War, many voices were still clamoring for abolition. In 1880, the Spanish Crown finally gave in. A law was passed that abolished slavery, but for many slaves, little difference was evident in their lives, as all slaves who had not fought in the wars were still required to work for their masters in an indentured servitude for little or no pay for the next eight years. Considering the short lifespan of sugar slaves, this meant that many slaves would die without tasting the freedom the law had "granted" them.

However, they did not end up serving the full eight years. In 1886, slavery was completely abolished at long last. Cuba's sugar and tobacco were no longer made with blood. The black population was still generally shunned and not provided the same opportunities as everyone else, but at least they had something—freedom. And after three hundred years and many generations of slavery, freedom tasted very sweet indeed.

Chapter 6 – Freedom

"I dream with my eyes
open and always, by day
and night, I dream..."

- From "Waking Dream" by José Martí

José Martí had been dreaming of an independent Cuba since he was
a teenager. He was only sixteen when his poems were appearing in
print; some were the fairly typical love poetry of the time, but others
rang with patriotism and cried out for freedom. There was never any
doubt that Martí was talented, and he chose to use that talent in order
to further the cause of Cuban independence.

During the Ten Years' War, Martí published and wrote for *La Patria
Libre*, a pro-Cuban newspaper that supported the rebel cause. He
was arrested in 1869 and deported to Spain in 1871, returning to
Cuba in 1878 after the end of the war.

He wasn't able to stay in his homeland for long, however. During the
Little War, he was once again arrested for conspiracy and forced to
flee the country, finally settling in New York City in 1881. But he
wasn't finished with Cuba yet. Martí was planning another

uprising—and with the lessons learned from the Ten Years' and Little Wars, he was confident that this time they could be successful.

The Rewarding Truce

After the Little War, Cuba entered into an era of economic change. With so many slaves freed, the sugar industry was forced to change significantly. The number of plantations decreased; they had to be run more efficiently, and so the larger and more successful plantations grew and prospered while the smaller ones that had been dependent on slave labor gradually died out. The urban middle class grew, as did the working class with the addition of so many freed slaves.

The United States began to take notice of Cuba's riches, and U.S. citizens started to invest in Cuban land, particularly sugar and tobacco plantations. The island became so important to the U.S. economy that there was talk of Cuba being annexed by the United States. They had already taken Hawaii, and the same thing was in danger of happening to Cuba.

But Martí would have none of it. Working in Florida and elsewhere in the South of the United States, he was rallying exiled rebel leaders. Pushing for one more attempt at giving Cuba to the only people he felt had any right to it: Cubans themselves.

The Cuban War of Independence

Christmas Day 1894 saw three ships leaving Florida for Cuba. Each one was fully stocked with soldiers and weapons, but only one of them ever reached Cuba. The other two were stopped by U.S. authorities. One ship got through though, and it made its way to the island.

War was officially declared on February 24th, 1895. On March 25th, Martí presented his policy for the war in the form of the Manifesto of Montecristi. Building on the Cry of Yara, it called for a war that would treat the island and its people with respect, including respecting those Spaniards who did not oppose the war effort. The

Manifesto also strongly encouraged equality between races, stating that black participation was essential for victory. It ended with the resounding words: "Upon the shoulders of the black man, the Republic of Cuba has moved in safety." Little did Martí know that the war would be devastating for the island, its economy, and its people?

Inspired by Martí's words, Cuba responded in strength and numbers that nobody had expected. When he and other Mambi leaders arrived in Cuba in April 1895, they were met with an island in chaos. The rebels had taken Santiago de Cuba, Guantanamo, Baire, and other cities; the majority of Cubans supported the rebel cause, but there was one enormous problem. Following the Ten Years' War, Spanish authorities had forbidden the possession of weapons. The rebels had to make do with what little they could smuggle from the U.S., and they were forced to employ the same guerrilla tactics that had been used centuries ago by Hatuey and his men.

Spain was shocked by the suddenness and strength of the uprising. The Spanish army on the island was increased from about 80,000 to about 300,000, vastly outnumbering the rebels. A *trocha*—a broad defensive belt—was constructed across the island in an attempt to keep the rebels in the east; previous wars had failed because of rebel inability to attack the west side of the island and take Havana. The *trocha* was constructed of barbed wire and booby traps at strategic points. The tactic had been successful during the Ten Years' War, but the Cuban commanders were already familiar with the *trocha*, and they were prepared for it. It served only to slow them down, not to stop them.

Martí's death in late 1895, during a heated battle with the Spanish, did little to slow the rebels down. Instead, the heroic death of their leader only seemed to spur them on to greater efforts. By the beginning of 1896, they had invaded every single province on the island. Spain responded by replacing General Arsenio Martínez-Campos y Antón with General Valeriano Weyler, a man whose utter inhumanity would earn him the nickname of "The Butcher."

Weyler was given free rein to do as he would to crush the insurrection, and he immediately started to play dirty. Removing the peaceful rural population from the countryside, he installed them in concentration camps and destroyed their crops and livestock, a process known as reconcentration. Between the diseases that spread so quickly through the camps and the famine caused by this wanton destruction, Weyler is estimated to have caused the death of about one-quarter of the island's entire population.

His tactic backfired badly. Disgusted by his actions, the Cuban population turned against the Spanish army. Despite its huge numbers, the army found itself on the defensive as it struggled to find any support from Cubans and was hated wherever they went. The rebels were still unable to procure enough weaponry as both Spain and the U.S. stopped ships carrying weapons from reaching Cuba, but their guerrilla tactics were working. By 1897, the rebel force, one-tenth of the size of the Spanish army, controlled most of the island. They held an assembly in La Yaya on October 10th, 1897, adopting a constitution and naming Bartolomé Masó their president. Masó had been part of the rebellion since the Cry of Yara, and had been vice president since 1895.

Economically drained by trying to crush another uprising in the Philippines at the same time as fighting the war in Cuba, Spain was forced to start changing its government in an attempt to placate the Cubans. They, too, established a new constitution and sent new leaders to Havana. More importantly, it replaced Weyler and ended reconcentration. But it wasn't enough. Only independence would do, and the rebels were willing to fight until independence was achieved by any means.

American Intervention

By January 1898, Havana itself was in chaos. Riots erupted all over the city as Spanish loyalists protested the new government, burning down printing presses that had opposed the Spanish Army and publicized its atrocities. The violence was such that the United States sent one of its newly-commissioned warships, the USS *Maine*, to lie at anchor in the harbor in an attempt to dissuade the rioters from harming any American citizens.

The United States had been following the war in Cuba with interest. Although the U.S. Coast Guard had stopped ships from getting through to the rebels with weapons, newspapers were printing stories about rebel nobility and Spanish atrocity, most of them exaggerated. The public was already pushing for the U.S. to intervene in support of the rebels, so the Americans in Havana may have had good reason to be nervous. But the majestic *Maine* was more than enough of a deterrent; Americans were left well alone.

At least, those onshore were left alone. On the evening of February 25th, the *Maine* exploded. Almost three hundred of its crew was instantly killed, and the mighty warship sank in Havana Harbor, burning as it went down. For more about the explosion, see *A History of Havana: A Captivating Guide to the History of the Capital of Cuba from Christopher Columbus' Arrival to Fidel Castro.*

The American press went wild. Employing yellow journalism, two American papers, *New York World* and *New York Journal*, competed with one another to tell the most sensational story, whether it was totally true or not. Matters were only made worse when U.S. authorities concluded that the *Maine* had been blown up by a mine, most likely placed there by the Spanish. Despite Spanish protestations that this was not the case, public outcry forced the United States to declare war. The U.S. was still a relatively new power, fresh out of the American Civil War, and had not yet been proven in international warfare; it was hungry to flex its new muscles, and the explosion of the *Maine* provided the perfect opportunity.

The American people were baying for war, but President William McKinley was reluctant. However, under pressure from the public, he declared war in April 1898, a war that would be known as the

Spanish-American War. The army had been unprepared earlier in the year, having only 25,000 men, but the *Maine* changed all that; about 100,000 volunteers signed up the night after she exploded.

On June 22nd, the first American troops arrived in Cuba, landing east of Santiago. They were welcomed by the Cuban rebels, who provided protection for them and taught them their guerrilla tactics. Despite losing the Battle of Las Guasimas on June 24th when the Spanish caught them in an ambush, the Americans pressed on, aiming for their main goal: Santiago de Cuba. But this city would not be taken by land forces. It would take a naval battle to capture it, and on July 3rd, this was exactly what the Americans did.

The Battle of Santiago de Cuba

Admiral Pascual Cervera was trapped and he knew it.

He had never agreed with this war in the first place. His many years of loyal service in the Navy told him that Spain couldn't possibly win the war against America anyway; the U.S. ships were far superior, its men better fed, and its economy not so depleted by decades of war as Spain's was. But when he was ordered to go, he had little option but to go, taking his fleet of ships to Santiago de Cuba for a battle that he knew would be fruitless. What else could he do? He was a soldier, and following orders was what he did. Still, it left a bitter taste in his mouth to be a sitting duck in the harbor of Santiago, knowing that he was about to sacrifice the lives of his men in a battle that he was confident they couldn't win.

American commanders, Rear Admiral William T. Sampson and Commodore Winfield Scott Schley, had already set up a half-moon blockade near the channel to the bay. Cervera had no way out, but he hoped that his commanders would allow him to at least attempt retreat out of the bay and into open waters where some of his ships stood a chance to escape. His fleet was lightly armed, and he knew that battling with the Americans in the bay itself was certain death. Perhaps if they could get onto the open sea then at least some of them could escape. His highest hope was for his new cruiser, the

Cristóbal Colón. She was well-armored and swift, carrying a load of Cardiff coal that he hoped would help her outrun even America's finest.

At last, on July 2nd, Cervera received word from General Ramon Blanco y Erenas ordering him to attempt his escape from Santiago. Cervera knew that it was all but impossible. Still, he had to try. Escape by night would provide cover from the Americans, but navigating the bay in the dark would be a dangerous mistake, so on Sunday morning at nine o' clock—as the American soldiers were engaged with church aboard their ships—Cervera attempted his escape. One by one he ordered the Spanish ships out of the harbor, leading the way aboard his flagship, *Infanta Maria Teresa*. By 9:31, they were within range, and the Americans immediately opened fire. Four American warships immediately began to fire on the Spanish fleet, shattering the peace of the Sunday morning; the white steam rising from the ships' engines was obscured by tar-black smoke as both sides started taking damage. Despite some initial confusion as the American ships almost collided with one another and masked each other's fire, soon the USS *Iowa* managed to punch two tremendous 12" rounds into the *Infanta Maria Teresa*.

More fire came from the fortifications alongside the channel, supporting the Spanish in their desperate dash for freedom. The *Cristóbal Colón* poured fire into the *Iowa*, slowing her down, as the other Spanish ships steamed to the west as fast as they could. The *Iowa* was slowed but not incapacitated; she engaged one of the ships at the rear of the Spanish line, the *Almirante Oquendo*. The foremost ships saw their gap and went for it with all the speed they could muster, and the American fleet immediately gave chase.

Trying to give his men time to escape, Cervera swung the *Infanta Maria Teresa* around and attacked the nearest American ship, the *Brooklyn*. It was a one-sided struggle that Cervera knew he couldn't win, but as the *Brooklyn*'s guns tore into his flagship, he hoped that the other ships could get away. It was a costly gamble; one of the first shots ripped the *Infanta Maria Teresa*'s fire main apart, destroying its fire control systems, and flame engulfed the warship.

The *Almirante Oquendo* was not faring much better. Fifty-seven direct hits had the ship limping; when one of her own shells detonated before it could be fired, her gun crew was blown to pieces. Her dying captain had her scuttled.

By 10:35, the *Infanta Maria Teresa*'s bridge crew was dead and she was all but destroyed. Trying to save the handful of men that were left, Cervera ran her aground at the same time as the *Almirante Oquendo* was taken out of the fight. The two Spanish destroyers were themselves destroyed not much later, the majority of their men dying; their other armored cruiser, *Vizcaya*, battled valiantly with the *Brooklyn* for an hour before she, too, was forced to run aground. Only the *Cristóbal Colón* was left. She was so new that she didn't even have a main turret yet, only secondary guns, so all she could hope for was escape. Only one American ship, the *Oregon*, could hope to keep up with her, and she steamed vigorously after the Spanish ship. It was a life-or-death race to the open sea, one which the *Cristóbal Colón* almost won. But finally, as the afternoon wore on, she ran out of her quality Cardiff coal and was forced to use poor reserves from war-torn Cuba.

The *Oregon* had almost caught up when the captain of the *Cristóbal Colón* decided that he could not escape and he would never win a direct battle with the American ships. To flee was impossible; to fight would be a pointless loss of life. He surrendered, and despite efforts to scuttle her, the *Cristóbal Colón* was taken by the Americans.

Despite U.S. efforts to rescue as many survivors as they could, almost one quarter of the Spanish fleet's men died. Of the Americans, only one did not survive.

Independence at Last

Assisted by their powerful neighbor, the Cuban rebels continued to push through the Spanish army, and the war was now as one-sided as the battle at Santiago had been. Even though most of the Americans eventually had to evacuate due to a devastating outbreak of yellow fever, American victories in both Cuba and Puerto Rico had decimated the Spanish force. After only ten weeks of conflict, Spain sued for peace. The fight was over at last.

The United States would continue to occupy Cuba as the rebels established their government. Although Cubans were almost entirely pushed out of the U.S. peace talks with Spain, and the eventual peace treaty prevented Cuba from making foreign alliances other than with the U.S. and granted the U.S. the right to establish a naval base in Guantanamo Bay, it would appear that getting American intervention had still been worth it. Because on May 20, 1902, it was made official: Cuba belonged only to itself. The fight had been won.

Chapter 7 – Independent at Last

On January 1ˢᵗ, 1899, after the last of the Spanish troops left Cuba, American John R. Brooke, who had been a Union general in the American Civil War, was appointed as temporary governor of Cuba. The Teller Amendment prevented U.S. annexation of Cuba—something that took place in Puerto Rico and the Philippines following the Spanish-American War—but many Americans could still use some loopholes to acquire land in Cuba. The country was decimated by war and poverty; land was cheap, and American investors saw their chance. Within a few years, the United States had practically taken over the Cuban sugar industry.

However, Cuba was far from becoming an American colony. In 1900, their first local elections were held. These were still not equal and free; while there were no restrictions on race, only men older than 20 years were allowed to vote, and even then, only if they were both literate and owned at least US$250 worth of property. At the time, Cuba's population was over one and a half million; only 150,000 were eligible for voting. These limitations were imposed by the U.S. administrations, who were hoping to force pro-American parties into office.

Their attempt failed. The cries of revolutionary heroes still rang in the ears of all Cubans, including that limited handful that were allowed to vote, and the Cuban National Party—a strong independent movement—won most of the elections.

The presidential elections were also somewhat manipulated. There were only two candidates for presidency: Bartolomé Masó and Tomás Estrada Palma. Masó had already served as president during the revolution, but the American administration found him independent-minded and opinionated, favoring the meeker Palma instead. Infuriated by this special treatment, Masó withdrew his candidacy, and Palma became the first president of Cuba by default. The Republic of Cuba was officially handed over to him on May 20th, 1902.

Uneasy Independence

The Cuban people had just suffered through decades of war to gain their freedom. They were immediately and entirely suspicious of anyone who so much as hinted at dictatorship or tyranny, and this was made evident in 1906.

Palma's first presidency was peaceful; he was careful with money and improved infrastructure across the island, although many accused him of being too dependent on and lenient with the United States. He had agreed to the Platt Amendment, which granted the U.S. exclusive rights to an alliance with Cuba and the right to intervene militarily should the peace treaty be threatened, which did not go down well with many Cubans. So, when Palma attempted to extend his presidency in 1906 against the constitution, the people revolted, and the U.S. military intervened to pacify the people and hold the first truly free and fair presidential election in 1908. This pattern of good presidential first terms followed by attempts at extending them and revolts by the people pacified by the U.S. would continue for the next several years. More on this time of unrest can be found in *History of Havana: A Captivating Guide to the History of the Capital of Cuba from Christopher Columbus' Arrival to Fidel Castro.*

For the average Cuban, however, life certainly improved on the island. Although foreign investors held most of the power, infrastructure was greatly improved, and despite the occasional small revolts, violence was hugely decreased. The Cuban people were able to start picking themselves back up again after the horror that was the War of Independence.

Cuba and the First World War

As Cuba started to find its feet as a country, the world was losing its grip on peace. Mario Garcia Menocal, who had been a military leader during the War of Independence, was president when World War I broke out in 1914. At first, still trying to smooth things out within his own country, Menocal kept Cuba neutral—something which most Latin American countries elected to do for the duration of the war. He had enough to deal with at home. Like other presidents before him, Menocal was reelected in 1916, and former president, José Miguel Gómez, led an armed uprising against him known as the Chambelona War. The uprising was unsuccessful, and as World War I raged, Menocal maintained his grip on his title.

The Cuban economy was improving during Menocal's presidency, in part due to high sugar exports; by 1917, it was the largest sugar exporter in the world, and at a time when sugar was scarce due to the war, this was no mean feat. Most of this sugar was going to the United States, upon which Cuba's economy was strongly dependent. So, when the United States declared war on Germany in 1917, Cuba had little option but to follow. German ships in Havana Harbor were immediately seized and given to the U.S. to use as they would; 25,000 troops were prepared to be sent to Europe, but the war was over before they could leave the island. One hundred doctors and nurses were sent into the war, however, to work in Allied field hospitals. No major conflicts ever occurred near enough to Cuba that the country was badly affected by the war.

The Dictatorship of Gerardo Machado

Menocal released his grip on power in 1920, when the population promptly elected President Alfredo Zayas. Zayas succeeded in serving a peaceful term, albeit loaning money from the United States when Cuba's economy suffered after sugar prices took an unexpected nosedive. The plan paid off; by the time Gerardo Machado was elected in 1925, the economy had been restored to the point where the ambitious new president could launch a series of projects in an attempt to modernize his country.

Machado had been one of the youngest Cuban generals to serve in the War of Independence. After his election, he promised to serve only for one term, but by 1927, he was amending the constitution so that he could be reelected. In 1928, he was elected for a second term—fraudulently, some suspect—and his reign of terror began in earnest.

A mild-faced man with neatly slicked back hair and careful little round spectacles, Machado achieved his dreams of improving the island's infrastructure by building the 700-mile Central Highway and expanding the University of Havana, but he struck fear into Cuban citizens by the violence that surrounded him. The people feared arrest above all else, as many prisoners were found inexplicably dead. Even more sensational were the numerous attempts on Machado's life. One such attempt involved the murder of the president of the Cuban Senate and the subsequent booby-trapping of his family crypt with the expectation that Machado would attend the funeral and be blown to pieces. Luckily for Machado, the dead man's family decided to bury him elsewhere instead.

Police violence was common during Machado's presidency. As the economy crashed—not helped by the Wall Street disaster of 1929—the people grew more and more discontent, and uprisings sprouted throughout the island. Machado's solution was to rule his people with fear, allowing his policemen to brutally crush all opposition. But he would not succeed forever. In 1933, foreseeing trouble, the

U.S. intervened, deposing Machado and instituting a provisional government with Carlos Manuel de Céspedes y Quesada—the son of that Céspedes who had first rung the bell and raised his voice for freedom decades ago—as president.

The Rise of Batista

Fulgencio Batista was angry, and it felt like he always had been. Born to a father who refused to allow him to take the family name, he had run away from home at fourteen and carved out a life for himself doing backbreaking, humiliating work. As a mulatto, he was a symbol of the melting pot that Cuba had become; his ancestry included the Taíno who had first loved the island, the Spanish that had so cruelly oppressed it, the Africans who had been enslaved upon it, and even the Chinese who had been indentured workers there as slavery faded. He was twenty years old when he traveled to Havana to join the Army and find an outlet for his rage against the world.

In 1933 that rage reached its peak. Sick of dictatorship, Batista led the Sergeant's Revolt, a military coup in which the army sergeants at Havana rose up against their officers and succeeded in overthrowing the government. Supported by the men under their command, the sergeants quickly overthrew their barracks. Sympathizers from elsewhere in the island rallied to support them, and soon they had driven most of the government officers in Havana away. Only two days after starting the revolt, the sergeants assembled a Pentarchy—a new form of government presided over by five leaders—and declared control over the country.

Batista did not immediately become president after the Revolt. Instead, a series of short-lived presidents were installed, but these were all mere puppets, and Batista, as leader of the armed forces, firmly held the strings. Only Federico Laredo Brú succeeded in serving a full term from 1936 to 1940.

In 1940, Batista finally ran for president himself, and he was promptly elected. He was about to face a baptism through fire as Cuban president though: a world war had broken out once more.

Cuba entered WWII shortly after the United States, joining the Allies after the attack on Pearl Harbor in 1941, which made it one of the first Latin American countries to join the war. Batista was faced with the daunting task of putting together an army on his tiny island, and he succeeded in shaping a tiny but efficient force, which was demonstrated in 1942 when his little navy found itself faced with one of the most dreaded forces of the war: a German U-boat.

The Sinking of *U-176*

The first Cuban merchant vessel sank on August 12th, 1942. *Manzanillo* and *Santiago de Cuba* were loaded with tons upon tons of cargo, heading past the Florida Keys on a trade voyage, when a German U-boat, *U-508*, launched a deadly attack on them, sinking both ships and killing thirty of the crew. These were rapidly followed by the wrecks of four more Cuban ships, causing the loss of eighty lives and more than ten thousand tons of cargo. Two of these ships were sunk by one notorious German submarine: *U-176*.

May 15th, 1943 saw two more merchant ships approaching Havana with trepidation. One was Cuban, the other Honduran, and they were both carrying crews on high alert. The sinking of the other ships was still fresh in their minds, and the presence of a squadron of submarine chasers for protection did little to allay their fears.

Mario Ramirez Delgado was commander of the CS-13, the submarine chaser bringing up the rear of the convoy. The CS-13 was fast and well-armed, and Delgado kept a sharp eye on the sonar, keen to get back at the Germans that had taken so many Cuban lives. And at a quarter past five that evening, he would get his chance.

It was an American plane that spotted *U-176* first. Flying southwest, the plane spotted the submarine lurking near the Cuban convoy, and the pilot knew he had to signal the submarine chasers to save the ships. Diving low, he circled his plane close to the waves, switching his engine on and off to give a clear signal. The squadron chief understood the signal immediately and sent Delgado to investigate. Delgado responded with alacrity, pushing the CS-13 to her best pace, with the sonar operator intensely focused on his equipment, as thirsty as his commander was for German blood. It was largely thanks to that sonar operator—an extraordinary Afro-Cuban man named Norberto Collado, a man who came from a poor background, but had an incredible ear for sonar—that the attack was so successful. He could hear exactly where that U-boat was. When a positive contact came back, the *U-176* was less than half a mile from the submarine chaser. CS-13 passed the submarine and started to drop depth charges from her stern, setting off explosion after explosion. Seawater sprayed in mighty columns into the air; the sea rippled with muffled explosions tearing the peaceful ocean apart. The closest explosion went off with a force that sent water cascading onto the stern of the CS-13. Then, a black bloom of fuel curled through the water, shimmering with an oily sheen on the surface. The *U-176* had been hit, and it sank, killing its entire crew.

Having arrived safely in Havana, Delgado proudly called President Batista to tell him about the sinking. While Batista congratulated the commander on his victory, it was inexplicably kept a secret from the public until the war had ended, when Delgado was awarded with the Meritorious Service Medal. The action was commended by other Allied countries as being an example of how efficient Cuba's little army really was.

The Batista Era

By the time the crisis of WWII was over, Batista was no longer in power. He had lost the 1944 presidential elections to Ramón Grau San Martín, who found his ruling over a Cuba that was riding a wave of high sugar prices and bustling, American tourism, causing prosperity to flood the country. Peace, however, did not go with it. Urban violence skyrocketed; gangs ran amok in the cities, and American mob bosses came on the heels of the tourists, opening hotels and casinos in Havana. Organized crime flourished, and corruption in the government grew. Grau was replaced by Carlos Prío Socarrás, who was even more corrupt and whose presidency was marked by violence between political parties.

When the 1952 elections were rocked by the tragic suicide of Eduardo Chibás, the leader of the Orthodox Party that aimed to combat corruption, Batista saw his chance to seize power. In another military coup—this one much less bloody than the Sergeants' Revolt—he installed himself as president, and the people were more or less accepting of him. It was a mistake. Batista became famous for starting an era of crime, corruption, and violence in Cuba, particularly in Havana. While the economy absolutely boomed, those who were getting rich were the rich, famous, and corrupt; the working class suffered. Much of Cuba's wealth was going to America as Batista continued to strengthen his alliance with the United States. Violent criminals and violent police alike terrorized the average citizen. As gangsters and movie stars rubbed shoulders in the extravagant Havana nightlife, unemployment was rife among the common citizens, with young people fresh from university unable to find work. The people were becoming increasingly discontent as Batista and his mobster friends, Meyer Lanksy among them, lived in the lap of luxury while the ordinary people struggled.

The time was ripe for yet another revolution. This one would last six years, and its impact would last for decades, providing Cuba with stability for the first time in centuries. The time of Fidel Castro was at hand.

Chapter 8 – A New Leader

Illustration 3: Che Guevara (left) and Fidel Castro (right)

July 26th, 1953. The date would become a legend; the name of the ultimate revolutionary movement in Cuba's long history of rebellion, the 26th of July Movement. It was seen as a battle cry for the oppressed, a beacon for those seeking change, a thorn in the side of authority, and finally—in decades to come—a national holiday. But right now, it was just a summer morning in the Oriente Province, the day after the Festival of St. James, when most of Santiago's inhabitants were still sleeping off their wild night. Even the soldiers in the Moncada Barracks were mostly hungover or still a little tipsy as dawn broke at 6:00 a.m.—or at least, so the rebels hoped. Fidel Castro's plan depended on it.

Not that the plan was going all that well. By the time the rebels had reached the small farm Castro had rented near the barracks, everything that could have gone wrong had gone wrong. Castro was forced to swallow his irritation as he supplied them with uniforms and weapons from his stash on the farm and briefed them on what they were about to do. Simply put, the convoy of seventeen cars was to rush the Moncada Barracks while the soldiers slept, and, keeping the fight as bloodless as possible, seize the barracks. Clearing out all the weapons they needed, they were to be gone before backup could arrive from elsewhere. These weapons were to start an army, and the army was to start an insurgency that would overthrow the corrupt Batista.

The attack hadn't started well. The plan was perfect: the rebels would travel to Santiago along with the crowds flocking in for the holiday, and then the car convoy would drive around the city picking them up early in the morning while everyone was asleep. But flat tires and lost drivers plagued them, and Castro was tense by the time they left the farm at 4:00 a.m. in three divisions. One, the largest and consisting of the most inexperienced men, was led by Fidel towards the barracks; another, including two female revolutionaries, headed for the Saturnino Lora Hospital; and the third, led by Fidel's brother Raul, made its way towards the Palace of Justice. In total, more than 150 soldiers were involved in the attack. The barracks alone held 400 soldiers. The plan could only have worked if everything went perfectly, and nothing went perfectly.

Castro's own mistake led to the complete disintegration of the plan. He crashed his car, allegedly smashing it into the gate of the barracks because the soldiers guarding it had realized what was going on; the ruckus woke the soldiers inside the barracks, the alarm sounded, and the shooting began. Half of the rebels in the first car were killed in seconds. Dismayed, Castro had no choice but to order a retreat, and as his men scattered, the soldiers gave chase.

Many of the rebels were captured and later massacred without mercy, their bodies dragged back outside the barracks to make it look like they were killed in the struggle. Fidel Castro escaped briefly into the countryside. Luckily for him, the public didn't buy Batista's story of how the rebel prisoners had been killed; they knew they had been murdered outright. By the time Castro was captured, the fiasco had become highly publicized. In a bid to win back some of the public's trust and support, Batista decided to keep Castro's trial just as publicized to show the people that the rebel leader was being treated "fairly."

The plan would massively backfire. Castro wasn't beaten yet.

Who Was Fidel Castro?

Born to a sugar farmer in the Oriente Province in 1926, Fidel Castro had grown up almost without a family. He was only six years old when he was sent to live with his teacher, then bounced from boarding school to boarding school until he finally landed in the University of Havana, where he studied law. It was during his time in Havana that the young Castro began to take an interest in politics. His first leadership role was as president of the Federation of University Students, where he immediately began to speak out against the corrupt and violent regime, and about how deeply Cuba had found itself in Uncle Sam's pocket.

Student violence was rife at the time, with a *gangsterismo* culture dominating the university. In an attempt to crush it, President Grau made gang leaders into police officers, and Castro was forced to arm himself and his friends for protection. It was his first taste of a violence that would follow him around for the rest of his life.

Castro was a member of the Party of the Cuban People when Eduardo Chibás took his own life before the 1952 elections. It was fuel on the fire. He attempted all legal and nonviolent means to overthrow the Batista regime, and they all failed. In Castro's mind, there was only one option left: armed revolution. He planned the July 26th attack on the Moncada Barracks, and on October 16th, 1953, he found himself in front of the cameras and the judge, called upon to defend his actions.

History Will Absolve Me

Castro was offered little legal aid, but he elected to defend himself anyway, drawing on his education, passion, and natural charisma to produce a four-hour speech that would later be known as "History Will Absolve Me" and became the political manifesto of the revolution. Batista's attempt to cow Castro into silence by the public trial failed miserably and completely. Instead, Castro catapulted himself into the public imagination as a tragic hero. He knew that there was no way that he could ever win the trial, but he did not let that slow him down in the slightest. Instead of being a sorry attempt at getting out of a prison sentence that Castro must have known was inevitable, he turned his speech into his first address to a country that would later become his own.

"I warn you, I am just beginning!" Castro stated. "If there is in your hearts a vestige of love for your country, love for humanity, love for justice, listen carefully. I know that I will be silenced for many years; I know that the regime will try to suppress the truth by all possible means; I know that there will be a conspiracy to bury me in oblivion. But my voice will not be stifled—it will rise from my breast even when I feel most alone, and my heart will give it all the fire that callous cowards deny it."

He finished his speech with an undaunted flourish that forever embedded him in the mind of the average Cuban. "Condemn me. It does not matter," he said. "History will absolve me."

Condemn him they did. While nineteen of the rebels were acquitted thanks to their successful defense, Batista could not allow Castro to go free. He and his brother Raul were both sentenced to more than a decade in prison and sent to the Model Prison on the Isle of Pines.

Prison and Release

Castro and twenty-five comrades found themselves more or less together in the Model Prison. They spent their time wisely; Castro managed to get "History Will Absolve Me" published and distributed in Cuba in his absence, and he educated his comrades and himself, immersing himself in Marxist works that started to push him more and more towards the precipice of outright communism.

Meanwhile, in 1954, Batista held another set of presidential elections. They were nothing other than a sham to appease a public that was starting to realize they were being ruled by a tyrannical dictator. There was no opposition, and Batista comfortably maintained power, but the move did cost him something. Castro's supporters caused violent protests and lobbied hard for amnesty for the political prisoners on the Isle of Pines. Finding him utterly hated by the majority of his people and needing some good publicity, Batista agreed, and Castro and the other prisoners were released in 1955.

Mexico and Che Guevara

Upon their release, Fidel and Raul Castro left Cuba for Mexico. Batista, relieved, must have felt secure in the knowledge that the troublemakers were gone, but this couldn't have been further from the truth. Castro had not left Cuba in his heart. He was coming back, and this time he would be ready to face the might of Batista's cruel armies.

It was in Mexico that Castro met Ernesto "Che" Guevara, a man who was to become central to the approaching revolution. Guevara was a piercingly handsome young Argentine who had spent time working in the indescribable poverty and suffering throughout Latin America as a medical student. The horrors he had witnessed had broken his heart, and he felt that he had to do something—no matter how drastic that something would be—to make things right. His Marxist-Leninist political views lined up with Castro's, and he, too, believed that armed revolution was the only thing that would solve Latin America's problems. The two determined and passionate men were a force to be reckoned with together, and soon they had put together a plan to return to Cuba.

By this point, Castro already had a band of followers both in Cuba and elsewhere. Holding on to the stand he'd made at Moncada, Castro had named his revolution the 26th of July Movement, or MR-26-7, and stayed in contact with other members of the group while he was in Mexico City. Training with Che, he put together a small regiment of revolutionaries who were willing to attack the Batista regime. All they needed was a vessel to get them over 1,200 miles of ocean back to Cuba, and in 1956, they found just the thing: the *Granma*.

Granma

She didn't look like much to anyone else. Antonio Del Conde, a gun shop owner with a sideline of snuggling, had bought her as a project. Once a bomb target boat for the United States Navy, *Granma* was only sixty feet long and almost everything on her needed replacing.

The Castro brothers, Che Guevara, and their small rebel army had been enjoying Del Conde's hospitality for the better part of a year. Del Conde had helped to hide and feed the growing army out of respect for Castro, a man whom he would later call his big brother, but he had no idea that Castro was following him when he stopped in to inspect his banged-up new yacht. The moment Castro laid eyes on *Granma*, he was smitten, and Del Conde just couldn't say no to him.

In a few weeks, Del Conde and members of Castro's little army restored *Granma* and made plans to undertake a voyage that was stupid at best and doomed at worst: the trek from Mexico to the coastline of Cuba near the Sierra Maestra mountains.

How exactly Castro and his army survived is unclear. For a start, *Granma* was only designed for ten people; she could carry thirty, at a pinch. Castro loaded her with 82 people. This meant that precious little food or fuel could be loaded, only the bare minimum being taken to keep the men alive. The weather was appalling, and it's likely that she would have sunk or stalled in the open waters if it wasn't for outstanding navigation and handling by helmsman Norberto Collado—that same Collado who had helped to sink *U-176*. He kept *Granma* on an almost dead straight course, a significant feat in that weather. They only made one detour, when one of the men fell overboard, and Castro, risking his entire revolution, turned back to find him.

Finally, on the second of December 1956—three days later than expected—*Granma* reached her target, crashing into a mangrove swamp under the cover of darkness. The men only had hours to get into the cover of the mountains before Batista's warplanes would find and shoot them down. Covered in vomit and feces from seasickness and the cramped quarters of the yacht, they plunged into the pitch-dark water, carrying their weapons over their heads, and staggered into the mountains.

Their suffering had only just started. When dawn broke, the abandoned *Granma* was spotted, and Batista's planes started to fire randomly into the forest. Only three days after the half-shipwreck, half-triumphant arrival of Castro's unlikely yacht, Batista's army found the rebels. A bloodbath ensued that cost the rebels more dearly than even Castro anticipated. By the time they reached the Sierra Maestra and the rebels began to find each other again, Castro was horrified to discover that most of his men were dead. As few as twelve remained: Fidel and Raul Castro and Guevara, as well as two female rebels, were among them. They had been utterly scattered during the fighting and only found each other by means of friendly peasants who took them in, fed them, and brought them together once more.

Breaking Point for Batista

Meanwhile, in March 1957, another revolution was attempted. This was as doomed and bloody as Castro's, as a student organization attempted to assassinate Batista and failed horribly, dying on the pavement by the Presidential Palace. For more details, see *A History of Havana: A Captivating Guide to the History of the Capital of Cuba from Christopher Columbus' Arrival to Fidel Castro*. The attack left not a mark on Batista, but it did horrify the United States, who finally recalled the U.S. ambassador from Havana and placed a trade embargo on Cuba.

Castro still wasn't done. By all accounts, he had been beaten twice, once at Moncada and now once in the mountains; but, he was hiding out in those mountains, growing his tiny army, gaining intelligence, and convincing the peasants to join him. Cuba itself was growing more and more restless. The more discontented the people became, the more vicious Batista's methods of controlling them were, and the more this drove them to dreams of rebellion. Soon, Castro's forces were strong enough to launch little attacks on small garrisons. They raided weapons from Batista's army and, piece by piece, their determination started to pay off. By late 1957, Batista was forced to take notice of their attacks and sent an army 12,000 strong to deal with the problem. Amazingly, Castro's army, numbering less than five hundred men, managed to throw them back again and again.

In August 1958, Batista's offensive had failed entirely; the mountains were under Castro's control and his army was moving relentlessly towards the center of Cuba. Batista's men found themselves on the defensive, trying to hang on to the cities as one by one the rebels fought them off and claimed the cities for their own. Guisa fell, then the Cauto plains in Oriente, then Yagajuey on December 30th, 1958. Their way was clear to Santa Clara.

The Battle of Santa Clara

Che Guevara's arm was in a sling, but he wasn't letting it slow him down. Santa Clara was in his sights, and he could taste victory in the air. His section of the rebel army was three hundred strong by now, and as they marched on Santa Clara, crowds cheered from the roadsides. They were welcoming a change from the Batista regime, and they knew that the fight was almost at an end.

There was one last obstacle, though. At the foot of the Capiro hill near Santa Clara, an armored train, sent by Batista in an attempt to reinforce his troops there, had established a command post. It was loaded with men and weapons, and Guevara knew that to take it would be a decisive victory that might just send that coward Batista running for his life. The first step was to trap the train. He commandeered a group of tractors from a nearby school of agronomy to start destroying the tracks leading back to Havana. Within hours, the train had been derailed, and its officers came out with their hands in the air, desperate not to fight these crazy rebels. As they negotiated, government soldiers started to wander over, chatting casually with the other rebels. They were growing tired of fighting against people whose cause seemed more just than their own, they confided. Like the men who had deserted their posts at Camajuani just the day before, they were done with this war. With very little fighting, the armored train was in the rebels' possession and the 350 men fairly peacefully taken prisoner.

Santa Clara was almost theirs. Marching triumphantly into the city, the rebels engaged the government troops that remained to stand against them. The force was almost four thousand strong and commanded tanks and bombers, but their fight was half-hearted, and there was only one casualty during the battle—although two commanders were executed by the rebels afterward.

Victory

As lunchtime passed on the last day of 1958, Che Guevara announced on the radio that Santa Clara had surrendered. It was the last straw for Batista. Even his own army would no longer fight for him, and he knew that the war was over. When day dawned on New Year's Day, 1959, Batista was nowhere to be found. He had jumped on a plane to the Dominican Republic, never to show his face in Cuba again.

After a long victory parade across the island, surrounded by adoring crowds who could taste change coming and hoped it would be for the better, crowds who had been inspired by a leader who had beaten an army more than one hundred times the size of his own, Fidel Castro arrived in Havana on January 8th, 1959. Cuba belonged to him at last.

Chapter 9 – Castro's Cuba

Castro could not have been more different than Batista in his rule. He was determined to provide a better life for the average Cuban, but as his term wore on, it became more and more evident that his ideas were misguided, marked by a certain paranoia that could perhaps have been expected of a man who had suffered so dramatically and striven against so much to get to where he was when he was first made prime minister in February 1959.

Communist Cuba

Although at first Castro denied any claims that Cuba was becoming a socialist state, he embarked on a dangerous game of Robin Hood. Instituting land reforms, he started to redistribute land to the poor, taking it from the rich and from all foreigners, effectively stripping Cuba of any American assistance. The higher-up civil servants found themselves being paid as little as half their previous salaries, while pay increased and rent halved for lower-level workers. One by one, hotels and casinos owned by mobsters and even innocent private owners were taken by the state.

The news was not all bad, however. Castro's intentions in many ways seemed to be in the right place, as he poured focus into healthcare and education. Houses and roads were built, water and hygiene improved, but free speech was crushed, and any anti-revolution sentiment was met with violence. The CIA all was declared war on Castro by assisting in launching, the Escambray Rebellion, a long and violent struggle from the Sierra Maestra—those same mountains from which Castro had launched his revolution. It was crushed by the strength and firepower of Castro's army; suddenly, he found himself in command of vast numbers, and the power was intoxicating.

All this had to be funded somehow. Repulsed by the idea of approaching Uncle Sam for help after he'd seen Batista so closely allied with America, Castro turned to the other great power in the world: the Soviet Union. Like Cuba, it was strongly Marxist-Leninist, and it was in solid support of developing countries. The USSR started to pour funding into Cuba, recognizing the usefulness of this little ally right next to the U.S.

By 1960, tension between the U.S. and Cuba had escalated as Cuba aligned itself more and more with the Soviet Union, with whom the U.S. was "waging" the Cold War. The U.S. placed embargos on Cuban trade, as well as ceasing its massive importation of Cuban sugar. Castro promptly nationalized U.S.-owned sugar plantations and refineries, as well as refineries on the island when U.S. corporations refused to refine oil that he was obtaining from the USSR.

The explosion of the American ship *La Coubre* in the Havana Harbor, a ghastly replay of the *Maine* explosion that had started the Spanish-American War, was the last straw. President Dwight D. Eisenhower ordered the Central Intelligence Agency to overthrow the Cuban government by almost any means necessary.

The Bay of Pigs Invasion

In 1960, President Eisenhower authorized the CIA's plan to invade Cuba and overthrow Castro. Training camps were set up in Guatemala and recruiting began, primarily among anti-Castro Cuban exiles living in Miami. Many of them had been a part of the mass exodus from Cuba during the days and weeks immediately following Batista's fall, and they all had one thing in common: they wanted Castro gone.

In March 1961, President John F. Kennedy authorized the attack on Cuba. Despite being vociferous in his dislike for the entire Batista regime and calling Castro an evil that America had created for itself, President Kennedy recognized the threat that the island posed. However, with anti-war sentiment all over America, he wanted to make the invasion look like a group of anti-Castro exiles engineered it without U.S. support. To this end, the CIA painted their bombers to look likes Cuban air force planes before sending in the first air strike on April 15th, 1961.

The strike was a dreadful failure. The planes that the CIA was using were old bombers from the Second World War, and although they attempted to bomb Cuban airfields, they missed, leaving the Cuban air force largely intact. Instead of incapacitating the bull, the CIA had only made it angry. Castro leaped into action, sending 20,000 troops to the front. Meanwhile, the amphibious invasion went on starting on April the 17th, with the troops of Cuban exiles landing in the swampy area near the Bay of Pigs. They were doomed from the start. Photographs had been taken of the planes, and it became evident that they were American; Kennedy withdrew air support, and the 1,400 invaders were left to face tens of thousands of angry Cubans largely alone. Meanwhile, the Cuban air force continued to strafe the invaders, destroying their ships and killing many troops.

Cuba also suffered heavy casualties, including the loss of almost an entire battalion to American tanks, known in Cuba as the Slaughter of the Lost Battalion. But as April the 19th dawned damp and rainy on a battlefield awash with despair, it became evident that the invaders couldn't hope to win. Kennedy finally sent help in the form of six fighter planes, but even this was no good; they were late, confused, and, ultimately, shot down by the Cubans.

By the end of the day, the invasion was crushed. Thousands of American troops were taken prisoner by Castro, and only released when Kennedy agreed to exchange more than fifty million dollars' worth of baby food and medicine for them.

The Bay of Pigs Invasion was only the start of trouble between Cuba and America. A less violent but much more terrifying threat was about to rear its head. The Cold War was in full swing.

The Cold War

Two superpowers rose from the ashes of the Second World War: the United States of America and its NATO allies, and the Soviet Union and its satellite states. The powers that had collaborated to throw down Hitler now found themselves disagreeing profoundly; on one side stood the Marxist-Leninist Soviet Union with its communist ways, and on the other, the U.S. with its democracy and free press. Both powers found ample reasons to go to war, but the utter destruction of Nagasaki and Hiroshima had displayed the danger of the atomic bomb and with both sides equipped with nuclear weapons, the results of all-out war could be catastrophic. Humanity had become powerful enough to engineer its own destruction. If the Cold War burst into full nuclear war, it could have had apocalyptic implications.

Instead, tension simmered across the globe, erupting in proxy wars like the one in Vietnam. And as millions of Soviet Union dollars poured into growing Cuba, it was very evident with whom Castro was siding. Cuba was a semi-colony of the U.S. no longer; it was now its tiny, dangerous, nearby enemy. It may still have been in Uncle Sam's pocket, but now it wasn't a wallet of cash. It was a hand grenade. And the Cold War threatened to pull the pin.

The Cuban Missile Crisis

Less than two years after the Bay of Pigs Invasion, tension between the U.S. and Cuba peaked in a crisis that would grip the entire country in terror for a few frightening days.

After the invasion, Castro met with Nikita Khrushchev, the leader of the Soviet Union, asking him for support against America. He knew that the invasion was just a small taste of what the U.S. was capable of, and he wanted his powerful ally to back him up. Khrushchev agreed, and nuclear launch facilities were constructed all over Cuba—just ninety miles away from Florida. Considering that some nuclear weapons had a range of thousands of miles, this was a frightening and direct threat to the United States.

On October 15th, 1962, President Kennedy was informed of photographs that American planes had taken of the nuclear launch facilities in Cuba. Kennedy elected to set up a naval blockade, preventing any ships carrying any form of weapons from entering Cuba. Tensions escalated over the next thirteen days. Despite being unable to get weapons to Cuba, the Soviet Union continued to send other cargo ships through the blockade, and construction on the launch facilities continued unabated; the United States responded by beginning to load nuclear weapons onto airplanes in preparation for all-out war on the Soviet Union. Castro was sure that another American invasion of Cuba was imminent and asked Khrushchev to strike America first, even though he knew that nuclear war with America would have resulted in the death of everyone in Cuba.

The Cuban Missile Crisis is the closest that the Cold War ever came to erupting into full-blown, worldwide war, which would have resulted in millions—if not billions—of deaths. Both the U.S. and the Soviet Union, however, continued to seek a diplomatic solution. Finally, it was agreed that the U.S. would remove its missiles in Italy and Turkey, while the Soviet Union would remove its missiles—which numbered as many as 192—from Cuba. The USSR did remove some of its Cuban missiles, but left the tactical rockets in place, which the U.S. didn't know at the time. However, none of the Cuban missiles were ever fired. Disaster was averted; the annihilation of one-third of the human race was avoided by a hair's breadth, and the world collectively breathed out.

The End of the Cold War

The Cold War would only come to an end when the Soviet Union finally collapsed in 1991. The entire world had been experiencing simmering tension for almost half a century, but somehow, nuclear war was averted. Thousands of lives were still lost in the proxy wars in Vietnam, the Congo, and other areas, but the world finally settled into peace as the Berlin Wall fell and the Soviet Union split into different countries, which gradually left the communist model one by one.

Cuba was one of very few countries that continued to hold on to socialism. And as their powerful ally crumbled to dust, the island began to experience some of its hardest times. With the U.S. still alienated from them and the Soviet Union gone, for the first time since it was discovered by Spain, Cuba was now truly alone. And true independence would cost it dearly.

Chapter 10 – Desperate Times

*Illustration 4: Horse transport in Varadero, 1994;
fuel was so expensive that many Cubans were forced
to use beasts of burden for transport.*

The United States was not the only country that was disadvantaged as a result of decisions made by Fidel Castro during his rule. Cuba itself also suffered considerably. By 1965, Cuba was officially a communist country; this meant that most privately owned businesses—even those owned by the Cubans themselves—were nationalized. Castro immediately began to shape the country he'd just won into exactly what he wanted. Anyone who dared to speak against the revolution he'd orchestrated, or deviated from his social ideals, was in danger of being imprisoned. This included the entire community of gay men, as well as Christians, conscientious objectors, or political opponents of Castro. All of these groups were sent to camps called Military Units to Aid Production (UMAP). There, they were forced to work, with gays being subject to "re-education." Thousands of dissidents were brutally imprisoned, sometimes tortured, and even executed. While life improved for the poor, any who dared stand against Castro quickly found him just as brutal as Batista had been. As a result, about 1.2 million Cubans fled the country, going into exile in the United States. Cuban Americans make up an important part of the population in areas of the Southern United States as a result.

Castro's well-meaning attempts to improve healthcare, education, and infrastructure at the expense of more profitable industries also spelled trouble for the Cuban economy. By the 1970s, Cuba was struggling, perhaps because Castro was also pouring resources into other developing countries as his own country attempted to develop itself. Tens of thousands of troops were sent overseas to fight in support of other Marxist-Leninist groups.

The Angolan Civil War

The most important of these conflicts was the Angolan Civil War. In 1975, the Armed Forces Movement—a group of people from various African countries—overthrew the Portuguese prime minister, freeing a variety of countries from Portuguese colonization in an almost entirely nonviolent coup. But for Angola, this was not the end of the struggle. Instead, it would be thrown into a turbulent civil war that would last for nearly three decades.

It was largely fought between three of the rebel groups that had helped to loosen Portugal's 500-year grip on their countries. The first, the National Liberation Front of Angola (FNLA), supported a rebirth of the old Kongo empire. UNITA (the National Union for the Total Independence of Angola) wanted Angola to be completely independent. Finally, there was the People's Movement for the

Liberation of Angola (MPLA), a Marxist-Leninist organization (although it later switched to democracy). The three factions had worked together to kick Portugal out of their country, but now they turned on one another and started to tear their mineral-rich country apart in an ugly, drawn-out war.

Cuban Involvement

Seeing that the MPLA was struggling, Castro mobilized tens of thousands of his troops and sent them over to Angola to fight in the same continent where once their ancestors had bought, sold, and kidnapped one another. This time, black, white, and mulatto stood together to advance Cuba's ideologies by supporting the MPLA.

It had started in the 60s when Che Guevara helped to train some of the MPLA's soldiers in the guerrilla warfare that the Cubans had proven themselves to be so adept at. As tension in the country started to simmer and threatened to boil over into war, Angola reached out to Castro, asking for his assistance once more: they needed instructors to teach their inexperienced forces how they, too, could win a guerrilla war against vast numbers. Castro obliged by sending five times the amount of assistance that the MPLA had asked for.

By late 1975, the biggest power on the African continent at the time—South Africa—realized that the situation in Angola could get ugly and that it could spill over into South Africa. Thousands of troops were sent to invade Angola in support of UNITA, fighting explicitly against the MPLA. Some of Castro's instructors were killed, and he knew he had to do something. Armed with weapons sponsored by the Soviet Union, he sent 36,000 troops to Angola to support the MPLA.

Castro's opposition of South Africa ran deeper than just supporting a fellow Marxist-Leninist organization, however. At the time, South Africa was embroiled in apartheid, a brutal segregation of its many races that left an ugly stain on the history of that country. Racial relations in Cuba may still have been difficult at the time, but Castro was especially outspoken about his views on race, that all Cubans were Cuban regardless of their skin color. So, it was that his mixed army was to fight against the neatly divided South African one. And he sent them in tremendous numbers; at its peak, the Cuban army in Angola numbered as many as 50,000 men.

Finally, during the Battle of Cuito Cuanavale—a drawn-out struggle that lasted several months—South Africa and Cuba reached a stalemate. The Tripartite Accord, ordering the withdrawal of South African and Cuban troops from Angola, was signed in New York on December 22nd, 1988. The Angolan War was over for Cuba, but for Angola, it would flare up again and continue until finally UNITA leader Jonas Savimbi was assassinated and peace was made in 2002.

Cuban Involvement in Other Third World Conflicts

Angola wasn't the only theater of the war Castro was waging against democracy and capitalism. He also supported Algeria's efforts to liberate itself from France, including their border war with Morocco; the Simba Rebellion of the Congo; and even the cruel and brutal regime of Mengistu Haile Mariam, a dictator of Ethiopia who was famous for genocide and crimes against humanity during a bloody time known as the Ethiopian Red Terror. It is estimated that this period of political upheaval killed as many as half a million people. Castro supported this awful dictator simply because, like Castro, he was Marxist-Leninist.

The Cuban involvement in Africa was greeted with deep gratitude by its beneficiaries, but for Cubans themselves, it spelled disaster. And as the Soviet Union collapsed after the Cold War, it became evident that without their mighty ally, Cuba's economy was on the verge of completely falling apart. The island was about to enter an era of isolation, poverty, and famine the likes of which it had never seen before.

The Cuban Special Period

As communism fell apart in Eastern Europe and the Soviet Union came to an end, Castro found himself suddenly without friends in Moscow. While he stubbornly clung to his Marxist-Leninist views,

Russia was turning away from communism and moving towards something closer to liberal democracy. Castro refused to change, and Russia refused to support him. Piece by piece, it withdrew its assistance, starting by removing its support of the Cuban military. The USSR had practically funded Cuba's involvement in African civil wars; now suddenly Cuba found itself without help and horribly alone. The military was weakened, and this was just the beginning.

Trade suffered dramatically, as well. With American embargoes on Cuban goods, Cuban exporters were forced to trade their goods further afield, and the socialist bloc of Eastern Europe had been the perfect market—responsible for up to 85% of Cuba's trade. They had also been able to import essentials like crude oil from there, and now that trade was collapsing. Cuba was unable to sell what it had and just as crippled to buy what it needed. It was as catastrophic for the economy as the withdrawal of American interest and the installation of American trade embargoes had been, except this time, there was nobody else left to turn to. Cuba had no allies left and could ask no one for aid. The market only made things worse, as the price of oil rose and the price of sugar—Cuba's great treasure—began to fall. The U.S. began to tighten its embargoes, recognizing an opportunity to get back at its nearby enemy. If the U.S. could not beat the Cubans, then it would starve them to death.

By the early 1990s, Cuba was in desperate trouble. Food was so scarce that the government had to ration it, often inefficiently; sometimes families were provided with only half the food they needed to make it through the month. Nutrition was so poor that nutrient deficiencies reached epidemic proportions, and oil was so scarce that people turned to ancient forms of transport to combat the astronomical fuel prices. Horses and bicycles started to fill the streets of Havana once more. Livestock, however, were difficult to keep considering that much of Cuba's animal feed had been imported. Castro's stubbornness was costing his people their well-being.

Almost every basic necessity on the island was compromised. Electricity suffered. Public transport was almost halved. Thousands of asthmatics found themselves without medication and dying when a few puffs on an inhaler could have saved them. Factories closed, jobs were lost in the thousands, and the sugarcane fields—for so long the backbone of Cuba's economy, the treasure of the island— were plowed over and used to grow fruit and vegetables for a starving people.

The situation grew so dire that almost as many babies were aborted as were born. Even pets and animals in the Havana Zoo were killed and eaten by people desperate to feed their hungry families.

Castro's government used subsidies in a desperate attempt to help some of its people, but even the government was struggling to survive. Finally, in 1993, Castro had to bend his pride or watch his country starve. He began to accept a few donations from the United States. Castro also had to start cooperating with other countries, even if he did not agree with their regimes. He started to open up his country to tourists from other South American countries, and, finally, even to tourists from the United States.

Tourism was ultimately the salvation of Cuba. For so long, this jewel of the Caribbean had been a forbidden pleasure to Americans, and filled with fascination about this country that so nearly destroyed them, U.S. citizens began to flock to Havana and other attractions. By 1995, tourism was a more important contributor to Cuba's economy than sugar. Despite the fact that Castro was now calling the United States a primary culprit of global warming—capitalizing on the fact that lack of fossil fuels had made Cuba environmentally friendly—his relationship with the U.S. began to improve to the point that he offered Cuban airports as safe diversions for U.S. planes after the horrific attacks on September 11th, 2001.

Alliances with Venezuela, and a new alliance with Russia beginning in 2000, finally began to drag Cuba out of its horrific decline. The Special Period came to an end at last in the early 2000s.

The end of another era was also nigh. Fidel Castro was about to be defeated for the first time since the Cuban Revolution, this time by his own body.

Chapter 11 – A New Horizon

Fidel Castro was sick and very sick.

The hero of the Cuban Revolution was now eighty years old, and his once pitch-black beard was thinning and gray with age. His intense eyes now stared at the world from a deep setting of wrinkles, and he was starting to feel the strain of more than forty years of governing his country.

It was the year 2006, and Castro had to undergo surgery for a mysterious bleeding somewhere in his intestines. He wanted to believe that he would return to the presidency. He wanted to believe that after the surgery he would address tens of thousands of Cubans again someday, as he had done in Havana shortly after he paraded through streets lined with his cheering people, fresh from the last battles of the Cuban Revolution. But Castro knew, in truth, that this was the end of his career. With Che Guevara having been executed without trial by the CIA as he attempted to launch yet another revolution—this one in Bolivia—Fidel Castro could think of only one man he would trust with his beloved, torn, abused Cuba. It was his brother, Raul. Raul had been with him for every step of the Cuban Revolution; they had launched the 26th of July Movement together, been imprisoned together, fled to Mexico together, survived that appalling voyage on the *Granma* together, fought in the mountains together, and ruled together in the turbulent years that followed. Raul was reluctant to take the position of acting president. Perhaps he didn't want to believe that his aging brother was edging into his twilight years; perhaps he felt daunted by having to step into the shoes of a personality as large—albeit controversial and, at times, cruel—as Fidel's. Either way, he finally agreed to do it.

For two years, Raul was acting president; Fidel was still involved in many decisions, depending on his fluctuating health. However, by 2008, Fidel finally had to accept the fact that he would never be healthy enough to be president of Cuba again. After forty-eight years of rule, he stepped down at last. Raul was made president of Cuba.

Eight years later, Fidel Castro finally died at the age of ninety. Raul was left to govern the country alone for the first time. He must have felt the loss of Fidel keenly, but under his presidency, Cuba started to slowly climb back to stability. It was with Raul Castro as president that Cuba and America began to really improve their relations at long last.

The Cuban Thaw

As Venezuela's economy took a dramatic nosedive, Cuba once again found itself largely without an ally, and Raul Castro knew that if he didn't make plans to improve trade relations elsewhere, his bruised country could face another Special Period. He recognized that America provided a significant opportunity to create more revenue by tourism. Considering Cuba's close proximity to the U.S., it could provide a much cheaper and more convenient holiday than many other tropical destinations. In fact, Cuba is vastly closer to the United States mainland than one of the U.S.' own most popular tourist destinations: Hawaii. Hawaii is more than two thousand miles from practically anywhere, being one of the most isolated islands on the planet; Cuba, by contrast, is less than a hundred miles from Florida.

As America swore in its first black president, Raul Castro made plans to approach this man peacefully, moving to negotiate for normal relations between Cuba and the U.S. Pope Francis and Canada helped to facilitate secret meetings in the early 2010s. In December 2014, President Barack Obama announced to the public that he and Raul Castro were going to take steps towards mutual cooperation between their two countries. The first official step was taken in early 2015, when President Obama proposed removing Cuba from a list of state sponsors of terrorism, which also includes Sudan, Syria, and Iran. The idea was entirely unopposed by Congress, and from that starting point, relations rapidly improved over the next year. The American embassy in Havana and the Cuban embassy in Washington, D. C. were reopened. U.S. tourism to Cuba spiked, with thousands flocking to enjoy this tropical paradise right on their doorstep. Travel restrictions were loosened; for the first time, commercial airlines began flights to Cuba, and even cruise ships started to journey from Miami to Havana for the first time in fifty years. The postal service between the U. S. and Cuba was also finally resumed after almost half a century.

No American president had visited Cuba since 1928—a time even before Batista. But President Barack Obama was determined to change all that.

President Obama Visits Havana

Obama and Castro first shook hands at the funeral of the same champion for peace who had brought about the end of the apartheid that Fidel Castro had found so repulsive during the Angolan Civil War: former South African President Nelson Mandela. The gesture was symbolic of things to come. Decades after it officially ended, the Cold War chapter of history was finally drawing to a close.

It would end at last in May 2016, when Obama made a bold move worthy of the history books. Eighty-eight years since Calvin Coolidge visited Cuba, an American president was going to set foot in Havana. And it was not only Obama who made the trip. He was accompanied by his entire family, as well as a delegation of more than one thousand prominent Americans. They toured Old Havana in pouring rain and high spirits. While some Cubans opposed Obama's visit, it went off without a hitch.

Obama hoped that his visit would make reconciliation between the countries irreversible. As the Stars and Stripes flew above the mingled streets of Old Havana, hope ran high across the globe. Obama's visit was not just a symbol of rapprochement between Cuba and the United States. It was a symbol of healing across the entire world, as the earth at last began to heal from a century of global conflict and tension. Archenemies across the globe were starting to shake hands. The World Wars and the Cold War seemed to be over at last.

And while Cuba remained one of the world's last socialist states, differences were finally being respected. Cooperation instead of war was being used to facilitate change. It brought hope to the world, but whether that hope would be false or not still remains to be seen.

Conclusion

*Illustration 5: Racial diversity shown as a group
of people walk down a street in majestic but decrepit Old Havana*

Today, American tourists amble through Havana, awed by the
attractions of this unhurried capital. UNESCO workers carefully
pick at the ancient buildings, peeling back years of neglect and grime
to reveal colonial Spanish treasures that seem almost untouched by
time. Pre-1959 American cars, beautifully restored, roll calmly
through the streets. The entire country reeks of its layers upon layers
of history.

Cuba has endured so much turmoil. Hardly a moment's peace has come to the country, from the savage conquests of the sixteenth century through to the simmering nuclear threats of the Cold War. Now, as the world starts to make peace with itself, Cuba is finally experiencing something akin to stability. This little island that made a big difference in history is starting to reach out to the hands that are extended to help it. Yet still a hint of stubbornness—that same stubbornness that led Hatuey to fight a battle he couldn't win, that kept Luis Vicente de Velasco in the tower of El Morro as Havana fell to the British, that brought José Martí back to Cuba again and again until he finally died fighting for the independence of his country, that helped Fidel Castro beat a force more than a hundred times the size of his own—a hint of that stubbornness still remains. Cuba remains communist. While America has largely backed off, no longer attempting to force liberal democracy on its obstinate neighbor, most of the rest of the world has already turned away from the communist model. Cuba continues to cling on, proud, tenacious, fearless, and stubborn as ever. There are only five communist countries left, including China and North Korea, but Cuba has never been daunted by being outnumbered. Obama hoped that thawing relations between Cuba and the U.S. would nudge the country towards what he believed was closer to freedom, but there has been little or no talk of any real change.

Life has improved for the average Cuban, however. More and more businesses are being privately owned now. With Old Havana being declared a UNESCO World Heritage Site, tourism continues to pour into the island, and the economy is starting to rise again. Lifted trade embargoes have allowed Cuba to get a grip on its economy once more.

Eighty-seven-year-old Raul Castro stepped down as president in 2018. Fifty-nine years of Castro rule came to an end, and Miguel Díaz-Canel was selected by the National Assembly to serve in Raul's place. While Díaz-Canel still rules a communist country, he was born in 1960, the year that Fidel Castro took power. Díaz-Canel does not remember firsthand what life was like under Batista with Cuba being exploited by the United States. He grew up under Castro, and perhaps his eyes will be open to the failings of this heroic, but deeply flawed, leader. He is expected to continue to improve relations with the U.S. and proceed with economic reforms set in place by Raul Castro, who is still first secretary of the communist party at the time of writing.

However, it is uncertain whether improved relations will still be possible. After some of the U.S. embassy's staff fell inexplicably ill, President Donald Trump retaliated by undoing some of the reconciliation that Obama attempted. Trade restrictions were tightened once more; certain hotels and businesses—those owned by the Cuban military—are now off-limits to American tourists. Trump's decision was ostensibly meant to protect the Cuban people by weakening the government that oppresses it through communism. Instead, though, the numbers of American tourists visiting the island have dropped, hurting businesses owned by those same ordinary people that Trump hopes to assist.

The hopes that were so high for reconciliation in 2016 feel a little dashed now. It remains to be seen whether Trump's actions will ultimately result in the demise of one of the last communist regimes left on earth.

For now, Cuba remains itself; controversial, at times violent, always beautiful, steeped in history, proudly different from the rest of the world, with that difference costing its people much of their freedom. It is an island almost without internet, a place that was closed off from the rest of the world for half a century and is now beginning to realize that there is a world out there that's very different from home. One thing is for sure: while perhaps not in its economy, in its heart, Cuba is truly independent. It has been a long journey to reach this point, a journey steeped in violence, but it can be truthfully said that—at long last—Cuba is an island controlled by no other nation. And island unlike any other nation.

Here's another Captivating History book that you might be interested in

Check out more books by Captivating History by going to:

https://www.amazon.com/author/captivatinghistory

Free Bonus from Captivating History (Available for a Limited time)

Hi History Lovers!

Now you have a chance to join our exclusive history list so you can get your first history ebook for free as well as discounts and a potential to get more history books for free! Simply visit the link below to join.

Captivatinghistory.com/ebook

Also, make sure to follow us on:

Twitter: @Captivhistory

Facebook: Captivating History:@captivatinghistory

Sources

Turnbull, David. *Travels in the West: Cuba: With Notices of Porto Rico, and the Slave Trade.*

https://www.globalsecurity.org/military/world/cuba/indigenous.htm

https://en.wikipedia.org/wiki/Guanahatabey

http://www.historyofcuba.com/history/oriente/tainos.htm

https://en.wikipedia.org/wiki/Batey_%28game%29

https://en.wikipedia.org/wiki/Macana

http://georgiegirl120.tripod.com/puertorico/id10.html

https://en.wikipedia.org/wiki/Ciboney

http://www.historyguide.org/earlymod/columbus.html

https://en.wikipedia.org/wiki/Sebasti%C3%A1n_de_Ocampo

https://en.wikipedia.org/wiki/Voyages_of_Christopher_Columbus#First_voyage

http://www.cubanocuba.com/hatuey/

http://www.historyofcuba.com/history/oriente/hatuey.htm

https://en.wikipedia.org/wiki/Hatuey

https://en.historylapse.org/colonization-of-cuba#spanish-conquest

http://academic.udayton.edu/health/syllabi/tobacco/history.htm

http://www.sucrose.com/lhist.html

https://en.wikipedia.org/wiki/Middle_Passage

http://abolition.e2bn.org/slavery_44.html

http://www.discoveringbristol.org.uk/slavery/people-involved/enslaved-people/enslaved-africans/transatlantic-slave-trade/

https://www.sahistory.org.za/topic/atlantic-slave-trade

http://abolition.e2bn.org/slavery_44.html

http://www.afrocubaweb.com/eugenegodfried/diegobosch.htm

https://atlantablackstar.com/2015/02/05/10-things-you-didnt-know-about-the-enslavement-of-black-people-in-cuba/5/

http://www.countriesquest.com/caribbean/cuba/history/spanish_rule/sugar_and_slaves.htm

https://en.wikipedia.org/wiki/Slavery_in_Cuba

http://pirates.hegewisch.net/havana.html

http://thehistoryjunkie.com/piracy-in-the-caribbean/

https://en.wikipedia.org/wiki/Fran%C3%A7ois_le_Clerc

https://en.wikipedia.org/wiki/Castillo_de_San_Pedro_de_la_Roca

https://en.wikipedia.org/wiki/Christopher_Myngs

https://en.wikipedia.org/wiki/Robert_Jenkins_%28master_mariner%29

https://en.wikipedia.org/wiki/Invasion_of_Cuba_%281741%29

https://www.britannica.com/topic/Spanish-treasure-fleet

https://www.history.com/topics/france/seven-years-war

https://www.britannica.com/event/War-of-Jenkins-Ear

https://en.wikipedia.org/wiki/War_of_the_Austrian_Succession#The _West_Indies

https://en.wikipedia.org/wiki/Sir_Charles_Knowles,_1st_Baronet

http://www.vaguelyinteresting.co.uk/12-october-1748-battle-for-havana-in-the-war-of-jenkins-ear/

http://central.gutenberg.org/articles/battle_of_havana_%281748%29

http://www.1066.co.nz/Mosaic%20DVD/whoswho/text/Battle_of_H avana_1748[1].htm

https://en.wikipedia.org/wiki/Battle_of_Santiago_de_Cuba_%28174 8%29

https://en.wikipedia.org/wiki/Battle_of_Havana_%281748%29

https://en.wikipedia.org/wiki/David_Turnbull_%28abolitionist%29

https://en.wikipedia.org/wiki/Year_of_the_Lash

https://www.encyclopedia.com/humanities/encyclopedias-almanacs-transcripts-and-maps/la-escalera-conspiracy

https://muse.jhu.edu/article/655218

https://findery.com/heather/notes/october-10-1868-carlos-manuel-de-cspedes-made-the-grito-de-yara-cry-of-yara

https://en.wikipedia.org/wiki/Mambises

https://en.wikipedia.org/wiki/Francisco_Vicente_Aguilera

https://en.wikipedia.org/wiki/Carlos_Manuel_de_C%C3%A9spedes

http://www.cubahistory.org/en/the-fight-for-independence/ten-years-war-1868-1878.html

http://www.latinamericanstudies.org/1868/Ten_Years_War.pdf

https://en.wikipedia.org/wiki/Little_War_%28Cuba%29

http://www.historyofcuba.com/history/race/EndSlave.htm

https://www.biography.com/people/jos%C3%A9-mart%C3%AD-20703847

https://www.thoughtco.com/biography-of-jose-marti-2136381

https://bombmagazine.org/articles/two-poems-74/

https://www.britannica.com/event/Cuban-Independence-Movement?anchor=ref130197

https://www.encyclopedia.com/humanities/encyclopedias-almanacs-transcripts-and-maps/cuba-war-independence

http://www.cubahistory.org/en/the-fight-for-independence/independence-war-1895-1898.html

https://en.wikipedia.org/wiki/Battle_of_Santiago_de_Cuba

https://en.wikipedia.org/wiki/Manifesto_of_Montecristi

https://en.wikipedia.org/wiki/Spanish%E2%80%93American_War

https://en.wikipedia.org/wiki/Cuban_local_elections,_1900

http://histclo.com/country/la/cuba/hist/rep/chir-ww1.html

https://jfredmacdonald.com/worldwarone1914-1918/latinamerica-18cubas-part.html

https://en.wikipedia.org/wiki/Cuba_during_World_War_1

https://en.wikipedia.org/wiki/Gerardo_Machado

https://www.iww.org/history/library/Dolgoff/cuba/6

http://www.historyofcuba.com/history/batista.htm

https://en.wikipedia.org/wiki/Cuba_during_World_War_II

https://www.thoughtco.com/cuban-assault-on-the-moncada-barracks-2136362

http://www.lahabana.com/guide/july-26-1953-attack-moncada-barracks/

http://www.cubahistory.org/en/corruption-a-coups/attack-on-moncada-barracks.html

https://en.wikipedia.org/wiki/Republic_of_Cuba_%281902%E2%80%931959%29

https://en.wikisource.org/wiki/History_Will_Absolve_Me

http://www.bbc.co.uk/history/historic_figures/guevara_che.shtml

https://www.thevintagenews.com/2017/04/21/granma-yacht-the-vessel-which-brought-the-cuban-revolution-in-cuba/

https://www.passagemaker.com/trawler-news/granma-yacht-changed-history

https://en.wikipedia.org/wiki/Cuban_Revolution

https://en.wikipedia.org/wiki/Fulgencio_Batista

https://www.jfklibrary.org/JFK/JFK-in-History/The-Bay-of-Pigs.aspx

https://www.history.com/topics/cold-war/bay-of-pigs-invasion

https://en.wikipedia.org/wiki/Cuban_Missile_Crisis

https://en.wikipedia.org/wiki/Cold_War

http://www.historynet.com/cuban-fighters-angolas-civil-war.htm

https://www.sahistory.org.za/article/angolan-civil-war-1975-2002-brief-history

https://en.wikipedia.org/wiki/Special_Period

http://www.historyofcuba.com/history/havana/lperez2.htm

http://www.cubahistory.org/en/special-period-a-recovery.html

https://forgingsignificance.com/cuban-special-period/

https://en.wikipedia.org/wiki/Fidel_Castro

https://www.dw.com/en/obama-makes-history-with-havana-visit/a-19130225

https://www.bostonglobe.com/news/bigpicture/2016/03/24/president-obama-visit-cuba/DsPp60xmrgAPlVHjpjV6lM/story.html

https://www.theguardian.com/world/2016/mar/20/barack-obama-cuba-visit-us-politics-shift-public-opinion-diplomacy

https://www.bbc.com/news/world-latin-america-30524560

https://www.economist.com/graphic-detail/2016/03/18/cuban-thaw-a-history-of-us-cuban-relations

https://en.wikipedia.org/wiki/Cuban_thaw

https://en.wikipedia.org/wiki/History_of_Cuba

https://en.wikipedia.org/wiki/Miguel_D%C3%ADaz-Canel

http://theconversation.com/cubas-new-president-what-to-expect-of-miguel-diaz-canel-95187

https://www.thoughtco.com/communist-countries-overview-1435178

http://www.yourlanguageguide.com/life-in-cuba.html

https://www.independent.co.uk/news/world/americas/us-politics/trump-cuba-travel-restrictions-what-does-it-mean-obama-rollback-expert-explained-a7794226.html

https://www.miamiherald.com/news/nation-world/world/americas/cuba/article213209104.html

Made in the USA
Middletown, DE
25 April 2020